Passport to
Mission

Passport to Mission

Fourth Edition

Cheryl Doss, Editor

Erich W. Baumgartner, Jon L. Dybdahl, Pat Gustin,

Wagner Kuhn, Lester Merklin & Bruce C. Moyer

Institute of World Mission

General Conference of Seventh-day Adventists

Silver Spring, Maryland, USA

Cover: Flávio Oak/CPB
Cover pictures: Cíntia Martins/BSK/ Melodi T/Jean Froidevaux
Original page layout design: Robert J. Ritzenthaler Jr. www.RippleEffect-inc.com
Fourth edition layout design: Amy Rhodes

© 2017 by Institute of World Mission
General Conference of Seventh-day Adventists, 12501 Old Columbia Pike, Silver Spring, Maryland 20904
(301) 680-6711 E-mail: iwm@gc.adventist.org

ISBN 978-1-943507-09-2

Printed in the United States of America

Contents

Part 4 Living in a Different Culture

Part 5 Sharing Christ in a Different Culture

Part 6 How to Be Prepared

Preface

Mission. Missionaries. What pictures do these words produce in your mind? Thanks to our parents who kept us supplied with a semi-endless stream of mission story books when we were kids, our minds are flooded with mental images of pith-helmet-clad pioneers, courageous men and women, incredible challenges, and dangers all around. We see Hudson Taylor walking the byways of China dressed in the flowing robe of a Chinese teacher. We see Adoniram and Ann Judson in Burma, David Livingstone and Mary Slessor in Africa, William Carey and Amy Carmichael in India, and many more. We also see J. N. Andrews and his two children leaving for Europe as the first official Adventist missionaries; the Westphals, Stahls, and Davises spreading the "everlasting gospel" to Central and South America; the retired seaman, Abram LaRue, blazing the trail to Eastern Asia; and of course, the well-loved "Dr. Rabbit"—Eric B. Hare, who labored in Burma.

As Seventh-day Adventist Christians in the twenty-first century, we need to realize we have received an incredible mission heritage. We stand on the shoulders of thousands of men and women who accepted Jesus' challenge to "go into all the world." They heard. They went. And their efforts were blessed.

As we at the Institute of World Mission have worked on the writing of this revision of *Passport to Mission*, a preparation manual for mission service, it has been with the prayer that you and others will be better prepared to follow in the footsteps of those missionary giants of the past—building on their successes and learning from their struggles.

And now as you begin your journey through this course, we pray that God will pour out His Holy Spirit on you and enable you to grasp the reality of what is ahead of you—the joy, the adventure, the challenge. May God bless you as you prepare to "Go" in response to His commission.

Institute of World Mission

General Conference of Seventh-day Adventists

Acknowledgments

As the number of short-term missionaries skyrocketed in the 1990s, the need to provide training materials for missionary volunteers became evident. In 1999, a concise but comprehensive training manual for short-term missionaries came into being with the first edition of *Passport to Mission,* written and published by the Institute of World Mission faculty. Volunteer missionaries sent out through the Adventist Volunteer Service office and colleges sending student missionaries now had the missionary training textbook they needed.

By 2002 when the second edition was printed, *Passport to Mission* was also in use as a textbook for the training of career missionaries at Mission Institutes. The 2009 revised third edition sought to update, expand, and internationalize the original book. Subsequent translations into Korean, Portuguese, Russian, and Spanish made the book accessible to an increasingly diverse group of missionaries. A fourth edition that updates statistics & references is now offered to answer the growing demand for a missionary training manual that meets the needs of Adventist missionaries from a wide variety of backgrounds who serve in a wide variety of roles.

This book would not be possible without the contributions of the original authors—Erich Baumgartner, Jon Dybdahl, Pat Gustin, and Bruce Moyer—and those who revised the third edition—Cheryl Doss, Wagner Kuhn, and Lester Merklin. Their insight and passion for mission have inspired and informed hundreds of missionary readers over the past decade and a half. Special mention needs to be made of the countless hours Erich Baumgartner invested in shaping and editing the first two editions of *Passport to Mission.*

The book in your hands, then, is the result of a collaborative effort of many people, but it has only one goal—the shaping of an Adventist missionary workforce that sensitively serves, generously gives, and wisely witnesses to the Lord of all.

Silver Spring, Maryland

November 2016

Part 1

Why You Are Needed

Chapter 1

It's
Urgent!

As college students, we remember thinking there were no worlds left to conquer. Richard E. Byrd had explored Antarctica. Hillary and Tenzing had climbed Mt. Everest, man had walked on the moon. There was nothing left to do that had not already been done.

Some people feel that way about mission. All the world has been reached and explored, they say. Whatever is left to do, the local believers can handle anyway. The day of the missionary is gone. There is plenty of work to do at home. There is no need to cross cultural boundaries to do mission.

We were wrong—dead wrong! There were plenty of worlds to conquer, we just didn't see them. Those who feel that the day of mission is over are also wrong—dead wrong! This chapter will show how far wrong this idea is.

 **Think About It**

- What do you think about mission and missionaries—are they still needed? Why?

- What facts do you base your answer on?
- Where do you get these facts?
- What do you think needs to be done to complete the job of taking the message of Jesus to the whole world?
- Who is yet to be reached?
- What strategy should be used to reach them?
- What are the reasons for your beliefs?

Look at the World

The Church is faced with many challenges in getting the Good News to the whole world. Some of these challenges are in the world outside the church, and some of them are inside the church. Let's start by looking at the state of evangelism among the more than 13,000 unique people-groups in the world. The immensity of the remaining task will quickly become clear.

The Non-Christian World

There are about four billion non-Christians today who have not been evangelized successfully. Nearly one third of the 13,000 people-groups in the world are yet to be evangelized. These are staggering numbers. This means nearly one third of the world's "nations, kindreds, tribes and peoples" have not been effectively evangelized! About three billion people believe in and practice non-Christian religions. Nearly one billion today are considered "non-religious." Look at the following chart. It shows the distribution of Christians and the main non-Christian blocs. Many of these people can be reached with the gospel only if someone from a different culture makes the effort to reach out to them. Only a minority of non-Christians live near enough to Christians to be influenced by them.

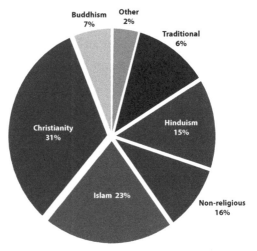

Figure 1. The religions of the world (approximate figures).

The Urban World

Since 2008, over 50 percent of the world's people live in cities. The remaining population is rural, heavily dependent on the cities. In the past, most megacities (five million or more) were in the western world and had an underlying Christian worldview. Today, most of them are in the eastern world and are not simply non-Christian, but often anti-Christian. These cities are an "Everest" challenge for Christian believers.

The Hurting World

Tremendous physical needs challenge us:

- Nearly one half of the world's population lives on less than $2.50 per day.
- About 35 million people have HIV; one to two million die each year from AIDS, including 200,000 children.
- Up to 150 million live as street children.
- There are 42,000 new orphans every day, many from HIV deaths.
- Over two million children die every year of vaccine-preventable disease.
- 500,000 children die each year from diarrhea.
- Six thousand die daily from drinking dirty water.

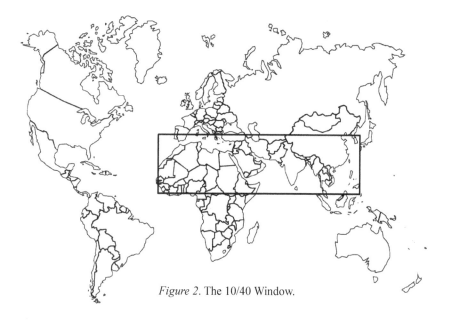

Figure 2. The 10/40 Window.

Nearly two thirds (63%) of the world's population lives in the area known as the "10/40 Window," yet less than eight percent of them are Christians. This part of our globe contains the area from 10 to 40 degrees north of the equator. It spans the area from North Africa through the Middle East and Central Asia to include the Asian subcontinent and most of the Far East. It is home to most of the world's Muslims, Hindus, and Buddhists. This is the least evangelized area of the world. Look at the statistics in the box below.

The 10/40 Window: The Least Evangelized World

- 72% of the people groups which are less than 2% Christian
- 95% of the world's least evangelized people groups (Groups where 90% have not heard the gospel!)
- 85% of the world's poorest people
- 34 Muslim countries, 7 Buddhist nations, 2 Hindu countries
- Fewer than 11% of all Christian missionaries work here

The 10/40 Window must be a priority in our mission strategy!

These challenges must be met by Christians if we are to be faithful to the command Jesus gave in the Great Commission. The 10/40 Window must be a priority in mission!

Barriers in the Church

As great as challenges are outside the church, the people of God also face challenges inside the church.

The Uninformed Believer

Many who claim the name of Christ are simply ignorant of the needs that exist in mission. They cling to some half-truths based on a few scattered facts. What many know about mission comes from a few half-heard mission programs at church usually focusing on the progress rather than the challenges. The church must be educated about the needs of mission.

The Distracted Believer

Money, busyness, and the world's everyday cares can distract us from our mission. Debt for an education and worry about the future can hinder our commitment to mission. Criticism of the church and its organization can also cause us to forget what we are really here for. Many don't deny the need for mission; they simply don't get around to doing anything about it.

The Timid Believer

Many of us are merely fearful and timid. We are afraid we don't have anything to share with others. Some are concerned about the response of others to a decision to go on a mission. Others are afraid of change or anything risky.

Who Will Reach the Unreached?

What does all this mean? Take a look at figure 3, which tries to summarize the magnitude of the missionary task today. It also lists four types of strategies needed to reach the different population groups of the world with the gospel.

God's Missionary Workforce

Figure 3 shows that the world population currently falls roughly into four disproportionate parts:

D World: Bible-believing Christians that take the Great Commission seriously. They represent about one tenth of the world.

C World: Christians in name only. No commitment to world mission. They represent about two tenths of the world.

B World: Non-Christians who live culturally and geographically near Christian neighbors. They represent about three tenths of the world.

A World: Non-Christians who can't hear the gospel because they live behind cultural and, often, geographic barriers. They can be reached only if World D Christians decide to send cross-cultural missionaries. The task to reach them is further complicated by the fact that they may live in restricted access areas of the world and often in utter poverty. They represent about four in ten people of the world. Most of them live in the 10/40 Window.

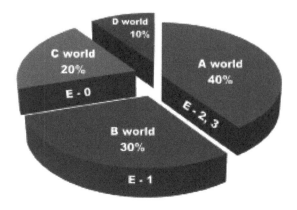

Figure 3. The unfinished task.

The Mission Strategy

Figure 3 also indicates four types of evangelistic strategies to reach different people groups:

E-0: Evangelism that brings revival to nominal Christians in a similar culture. It requires evangelistic tools for renewal and revival. Adventists are strong in this category.

E-1: Evangelism to unchurched Christian and non-Christian people in a similar culture. It requires sensitive evangelistic strategies that appeal to unchurched, secularized, and non-Christian people. We have had only marginal success in reaching people of this background.

E-2 and E-3: Evangelism across an increasing number of cultural barriers. Progress among World A peoples has been slow. Adventists have done well reaching tribal peoples. We are beginning to be more successful in communicating with people from the great world religions. But we still have a long way to go.

So What About You?

Can you see why ignorance about these facts is so serious? In this chapter a host of factors have been noted within and without the church that underline the urgency of mission today. Any one or a combination of the factors within the church can lead to a paralysis which cuts the nerve of mission. Some have been called by God to fight the challenge of mission within the church and by God's Spirit spark renewal.

There are plenty of mission "Mount Everests" still to climb. Needs are tremendous. Determine to boldly move forward, trusting in Jesus' presence, to meet and conquer these unconquered and unclimbed challenges for God.

Your Turn

1. Which of the challenges mentioned appeals most to you? What religion, area, need, or country is God laying on your heart? What are the reasons for this? What can you do now to work toward meeting that challenge?

2. Study carefully this chapter's charts and facts about the unfinished task. What strikes you most about the figures given there? Do you think most people in your church know these facts?

3. Analyze the people in your "mission field." Where do they fit into figure 3? How can they be reached?

Chapter 2

It's
Possible
Today!

Every missionary will face the question. Dr. Jon Dybdahl did:

The setting is still vivid in my mind. We stood at the view-point elevation looking over the beautiful city of Honolulu. Graciously our guide had shown us around the island, and it was now the end of the day. We had been together long enough to ask honest questions. "Why," he asked, "are you bothering to go to Thailand? You had a good church job in Northern California. You were near your family. Why throw that away? What is the value of going, anyway?"

If some of your friends and family haven't verbalized it, they have thought it. Certainly you have in your own heart and mind asked it. If you haven't, you need to. "Why would you choose to go as a missionary?" In this chapter we want to say emphatically, there are lots of good reasons to go. Let's think about them together.

 **Think About It**

- Who has asked you questions about the reasons and value of going on God's mission?
- What have they said, and how have you responded?

The Need for Short-Term Missionaries

We are defining "short-term" as any mission experience that lasts from two weeks to one year. The number of short-term missionaries has exploded in recent years. The number of people in short-term missions is so great, and the ways they are sent so diverse, that any numbers are "guesstimates"; but some have estimated up to four million short-termers of all denominations may be going every year!

The Adventist Mission Explosion

Student missionaries, Adventist volunteers, and ADRA project workers go in the greatest numbers, but numerous smaller sending agencies and local churches are also getting involved in mission projects. More short-termers go out from North America each year than the total number of regular Adventist missionaries now serving in cross-cultural situations (about 900) in the whole world.

The South Pacific Division uses some 1,000 volunteers on a yearly basis in short-term mission projects. And a few years ago Global Mission began to mobilize more than 1,000 local Global Pioneers each year in church planting projects.

To support this exciting trend, the General Conference established the Office of Adventist Volunteers at the Secretariat and several divisions also have an Office of Volunteer Ministries.

Why This Trend?

What are the reasons for this tremendous upsurge in short-term missions? Let us consider briefly three of the main reasons.

Reason 1: Travel and communication are faster and cheaper than ever before. Instead of taking weeks to journey to the mission field by ship, today we can be there in 24 hours!

Reason 2: Short-termers can give service—yet not disrupt the regular flow of their lives.

Reason 3: Churches and mission agencies now encourage short-term missions.

So What?

What good do these short-termers do? Aren't these just vacation trips for people who like to travel? What are the benefits to God's kingdom of all this going and coming? Consider the Benefits of Mission notecard that follows. What do you think?

#1 = benefits auself =
I isn't that backward

Benefits of Mission
Benefit 1: Mission benefits the goer.
- A broadened perspective on the world with all its hurts and needs
- A chance to test themselves and their ability to serve and adapt
- Realization of the benefits that come from caring for the spiritual and material needs of others

Benefit 2: Mission benefits the host people.
- They can see the caring and interest of the missionaries
- They gain new perspectives on their world and the world outside
- Spiritual and/or material aid is received

Benefit 3: Mission benefits the sender.
- Hands-on faith experience shared in the local church
- Greater dedication to mission and church
- Potential for future service at home and abroad greatly increased
- New vision for what the church can and should do
- Pool of experienced workers for more short-term/career service

An added important benefit is the benefit to a global church that is further united through real-life friendships that generate international, intercultural understanding and trust. The "communion of the saints" is made real as otherwise distant and unknown brothers and sisters talk together, pray together, eat together, worship together, and dream together—as they understand each other and love one another.

The Need for Career or Longer-Term Missionaries

Should everyone choose the short-term mission route to being a missionary? Of course not! Like everything else in life, there actually are some weaknesses in short-term mission:

- Since a short-term mission trip is often shorter than the necessary time needed to prepare adequately for mission, too often preparation and training are reduced at the expense of good mission.
- A short-term mission does not provide enough time to learn the culture and the language of the host people.
- Short-term missions are often driven by the results expected by sponsors, but the time spent is too short to do justice to the mission.

It is obvious that the Lord will be calling some to serve for longer terms—even making mission their "career." These missionaries will have the advantage of bonding with the people they have dedicated their life to serve. They will understand the culture better. They will learn the language of the people. The long-term missionary will, thus, be able to communicate the gospel much more effectively.

Look back at the list of benefits of mission. Do they not all apply to long-term mission, too? In many cases, the benefits will be stronger—especially if the career missionary remembers to stay in contact with the sending church!

Your Turn

1. From the list of benefits of mission which are the most important to you as a short-term missionary? As a career missionary? Can you add others to the list? What are they?

2. Do you think training is important for both long-term and short-term missionaries? Why?

3. Career missionaries or longer-term missions do have some advantages over the short-termers. What do you think are the biggest advantages? If you choose to serve longer in mission, what reason would you give for that choice?

Chapter 3

It's ªMandate!

There is more to being a missionary than just deciding to go on an adventure! Missionaries need to know certain practical things. Missionaries must learn to practice the nuts and bolts of getting along, communicating, and remaining healthy in another culture.

Something else, however, comes first. Missionaries are not worth much to God's cause if they don't know Whom they are working for and why. If those two issues are clearly in mind, all the practical training takes on meaning. This chapter and the next one are designed to do just that. Stay tuned.

 **Think About It**

- If someone asked you the biblical reasons for going on a mission, what would you say?
- What Bible texts are important to you as a prospective missionary?

God, the Missionary God

The first reason for Christ's command to go is that reaching out and blessing all nations has been God's concern all along. God cares. Remember, every person on earth belongs to the family of God—they are His children, and He loves each of them just as much as He loves those of us who know Him well. When God called Abraham many years ago (Genesis 12:1-3), He said that "all peoples on earth will be blessed through you." God chose Abraham (and later Israel) for one specific purpose—to reach all His lost and hurting children everywhere.

For reasons of His own, God has chosen to use us. He could use angels or dreams or other supernatural means, but He has chosen to send us to share with the lost members of the family (Romans 10:11-15). Jesus wants to use us to fulfill His original loving purpose to the world. This is not an option. It is essential. It's a part of being a member of God's big family. In addition, God has linked the Second Coming to the sharing of the Good News with the other members of the "family" around the world (Matthew 24:14).

The Great Commission

The text that many Christians have quoted to support their mission is Matthew 28:18-20. We call it the Great Commission. This passage answers seven basic questions about mission.

> All authority in heaven and on earth has been given to me. Therefore go and make disciples of all nations, baptizing them in the name of the Father and of the Son and of the Holy Spirit, and teaching them to obey everything I have commanded you. And surely I am with you always, to the very end of the age.
>
> Matthew 28:18-20

A careful look at this text tells us the essential things we need to know about Christian mission. This is Christ's last command to His disciples. As you study the seven basic answers, follow the text in your Bible.

1. Who sends us? — ye boi Jesus

The risen Christ is the One who sends—not primarily the church, the General Conference, our occupation, or anyone or anything else. This is what forms our self-identity. Our evaluation of ourselves and our work should depend on recognition of Who we are sent by.

2. On what basis are we sent?

The authority and command of the risen, worshiped Christ is the basis of our mission. Jesus has been given all authority and power, and He commands, not suggests, we go. Along with Matthew 28:18-20, see the passages in Mark 16:14-16, Luke 24:46-49, John 20:21, and Acts 1:8.

3. Who is sent?

The command is given to all the disciples who heard Jesus. The whole body of believers or the church is sent. The call is to the corporate group, rather than to an individual. Individuals need not wait for a special call, but as members of the body of Christ they are already sent. Rather than waiting for a special call to go, believers should ask if there is a strong, valid reason not to go. — Why not?

4. Who are we sent to?

We are sent to all nations. The term "nations" does not only refer to countries, but to "peoples" and ethnic groups. The world is seen as people rather than territory or geography. Christianity is a people-to-people movement. Earlier, the disciples had been sent to the lost sheep of the house of Israel, but now they are sent beyond the safe bounds of Judaism.

5. What is to be done?

The task seems to be outlined in four steps:

- *Go.* Depart from where you are and cross boundaries.
- *Make disciples.* A disciple is a student or learner. A student in Bible times lived with the master and learned from him, and followed and served him in all ways. We are to "make" these kinds of disciples for Jesus.
- *Baptize.* Baptism is the vital initiation ceremony and is in the name of the Trinity.
- *Teach to observe all Jesus' commands.* Teaching continues after baptism. One of Jesus' key commands is to go share with others. Disciples in turn are to become disciple-makers.

6. What is the source of power for mission? *— ye boi!*

Jesus promises to be with us always; this is the all-powerful, authoritative, risen Jesus Christ. His presence means that we are never alone. It also means He takes continuing responsibility for the success and progress of the mission.

7. How long does this mission last? *— till ye boi comes back*

The mission lasts until the end of the age. The mission is not temporary, but lasts until the end of this present age. Only Jesus' Second Coming and the kingdom of glory bring this phase of mission to its close.

So there we have it—the who, what, why, and how long of our special mission. It's a very powerful text! Did you ever stop to think about the significance of the fact that this is Jesus' last command to His followers? Parting words are almost always significant—things of special importance and urgency—and these were Jesus' parting words to His disciples. And we know He told them this more than once (compare Acts 1:8 with Matthew 28:18-20, Luke 24:46-49, and John 20:21).

As you know, this passage of Scripture is usually referred to as The Great Commission—a command. Sometimes Christians have wished that it was "The Great Suggestion" or "The Great Option," but Jesus' intent was clear: being involved in His mission to the world is part and parcel of being a Christian.

Now what do we do? What do we have to offer to the peoples in our own countries and around the world? And what does this commission mean for us as Adventists? The next chapter will take a closer look at these questions.

Your Turn

1. Using the ideas given in this chapter, briefly restate how you understand the Great Commission applies to you. What parts apply and how? Begin with the words, "Jesus said to me, '. . . ,'" and continue for about 50 words. What do you believe He is saying to you through this passage?

2. What other biblical ideas help you understand the mission of the church?

Chapter 4

It's Christian! It's Adventist!

In the last few chapters we've talked about several important aspects of mission, and in the last chapter we studied some of the biblical reasons why we go. We focused on texts that don't just suggest that we go, or present going as one of many options, but actually command that we go. But why is it so important that we go? What do we as Christians have to offer to the people of the world? Many people think we should just leave them alone and not bother them with Christianity. Others would argue that if we don't go and share the Good News of the gospel with them, they will be lost and it will be our fault.

 **Think About It**

- Why is it important for us to go?
- Why does Christ command us to go on mission?
- Why do we need Adventist missionaries?

What Christianity Has to Offer

One reason why we "go" is that there are some important aspects of Christianity that people need to know and experience in order to enjoy the abundant life here and now and to be ready to meet Jesus. The Psalmist said, "Taste and see that the Lord is good" (34:8). In reality, Christianity must be experienced to be truly understood. We will review here some of the basic beliefs Christians share. But we must remember that when introducing Christianity to non-Christians, we can't just string a list of Bible texts together to "prove" Christianity. They must experience God as a friend rather than just accept a list of beliefs. However, it is important to realize that our convictions are firmly anchored in Scripture. Let's review them now.

Jesus is the unique source of life and salvation and people need to know about Him.

- John 3:36: "Whoever believes in the Son has eternal life, but whoever rejects the Son will not see life."
- Acts 4:12: "Salvation is found in no one else, for there is no other name under heaven given to men by which we must be saved."
- 1 John 5:12: "He who has the Son has life; he who does not have the Son of God does not have life."

Jesus is the divine son of God. He does not claim to be just a good teacher (like Mohammed or the Buddha) or a great leader (like Moses or David) or some kind of half-god or lesser god (like Shiva or Krishna). No other major religion claims divinity for its founder.

- He claims full divinity—equality with God (John 8:58, 59; 10:30-33).
- His disciples also claimed His divinity fearlessly (Matthew 16:14-16). The proof that they gave for their claims was the resurrection (1 Corinthians 15:14-20). If God raised Him, what He said must be true.

Jesus offers a unique salvation—salvation by grace through faith.

- "For it is by grace you have been saved, through faith—and this not from yourselves, it is the gift of God—not by works so that no one can boast" (Ephesians 2:8, 9).

No other world religion has such a salvation. Others may have high standards, ethical behavior, health laws, a lofty philosophy, or nice people, but they believe that people can save themselves by what they do! The foundation of these non-Christian religions is that salvation comes by works.

Jesus offers a universal salvation—all-inclusive and exclusive.

- "For God so loved the world . . . that whoever believes in him shall not perish but have eternal life" (John 3:16).

Christianity is not an ethnic or national religion that belongs to one group of people. The offer of salvation includes everyone in the world! But while Christianity is freely offered to all, it is also exclusive in that it calls for a commitment that asks one to forsake that which is incompatible with Christian belief in order to become a follower.

The truth is that God wants all people to hear the message—the Good News message that God offers a free salvation based on this unique Jesus. In the Great Commission Jesus makes it clear that we can have a part in sharing this Good News with others.

What Adventism Has to Offer

Is there anything different and unique about Adventist mission to the world?

As Adventists we believe that we are to reach out "to every nation, kindred, tongue, and people" (Revelation 14:6). That conviction has resulted in about 19 million members in over 200 countries. What is the essence of the message that has driven this mission? What are we to share with the world?

 **Think About It**

- If someone asked you why you are an Adventist, what would you say?
- What reasons would you give for your belief?
- What Bible texts would you give?
- How would you relate the Adventist message to the unique Christian message we just talked about?
- How would you relate the Adventist message to the non-Christian world religions?

Remember that some statements and clichés we use to describe ourselves are not understood by those with no Adventist or Christian background. Though most of the individual beliefs of Seventh-day Adventists are shared by some other Christians, the "package" of Adventist beliefs is unique among Christian groups. We have summarized them as three convictions that guide what we believe and how we see our mission.

Conviction #1: Jesus is coming back again a second time—this coming is visible, literal, and imminent (soon).

Before Adventism got started, most Christians either did not believe in a literal coming or de-emphasized it. Many were postmillennialists. This means they believed that there would be a millennium or 1,000 years of peace and prosperity and then Jesus would come. What people looked for and labored for was this millennium, not the Second Coming.

Adventists believe, on the basis of their Bible study, that the real hope of the world is not a millennium, but the "blessed hope" (Titus 2:13) of Jesus' Second Coming.

- They read the promises of the coming: "I will come back and take you to be with me" (John 14:1-3); "I am coming soon" (Revelation 22:7, 12, 20).

- This coming is clearly literal. "This same Jesus . . . will come back in the same way . . ." (Acts 1:11).
- The coming is portrayed as visible. "They will see the Son of Man coming on the clouds of the sky with power and great glory" (Matthew 24:30). "Look, He is coming with the clouds, and every eye will see Him" (Revelation 1:7).
- All signs point to a near, soon, imminent coming. Jesus over and over used the word "soon" (Revelation 22:7, 12, 20). The signs Jesus Himself gave are being fulfilled (Matthew 24:4-28, Luke 21:7-28). The great prophecies of Daniel and Revelation pointed to the nearness of the coming. While this coming is bad news to evildoers, it is wonderful Good News to believers.
- They will see Jesus (John 14:3) and be with Him forever (1 Thessalonians 4:17).
- The dead will be raised (1 Thessalonians 4:13-16), and believers will receive immortality (1 Corinthians 15:53).
- Tears, mourning, and death will be abolished (Revelation 21:3, 4).

Our Mission Today

Today many Christians who are not Adventists believe in the Second Coming. This should encourage us to realize the persuasiveness of our position. Many, however, do not believe in Jesus' coming, or if they do, it is only in a partial or warped way. They need this Good News of the blessed hope. The biggest challenge we face, however, is the non-Christian world. Millions of Muslims, Hindus, Buddhists, and adherents of traditional religions have never heard of this hope. We must tell them. Jesus wants them to hear about His coming.

Conviction #2: God calls believers to loving obedience and serious discipleship.

In light of Jesus' coming we need to make serious preparation. Faithful, obedient discipleship is important. Adventists have always believed that Jesus is our Savior. Nothing we can do will earn our salvation. Only the free grace of Jesus enables us to become forgiven children of God. Our faithful discipleship does not build up merit points which gain favor with God.

Adventists have always emphasized that true faith is manifested in making Jesus also Lord. People saved by Jesus should gladly make Him Lord and in gratitude follow Him.

Before Adventism, many sincere Christians saw a conflict between the gospel of Jesus and the law of God. They believed that people saved by Jesus were free of certain standards of law. Some were lax in their discipleship. Adventists believe that both the gospel and God's law are vital and go together harmoniously like the two oars of a boat. The law leads us to Christ and serves as our standard. Jesus releases us from the law's condemnation, and His spirit writes the law on our hearts. For this reason Adventists—

- Support the whole Ten Commandments, including the neglected Sabbath fourth commandment, believing that
  1. Jesus gave it at Creation (Genesis 2:2).
  2. Jesus reiterated it in the Ten Commandments (Exodus 20:8-11).
  3. Jesus reinforced it during His ministry (Mark 2:27).
- Believe the Sabbath is a powerful symbol of
  1. God's creating power (Genesis 2:2, Exodus 20:8-11).
  2. Saving grace (Exodus 20:2, Deuteronomy 5:12-15).
  3. The final rest of redemption in heaven (Hebrews 4:1-11, esp. 9).
- Accept the Lordship of Christ in all areas of life, including marriage and family, dress, recreation, diet, etc.
  1. Husband, wives, children (Ephesians 5:21-6:4).
  2. Whatever is true, noble, right, and pure is good (Philippians 4:8, 9).

3. Your body is the temple of God (1 Corinthians 6:19, 20).

4. Dress and demeanor are important (1 Timothy 2:8–10).

Our Mission Today

More than ever, in a world where disregard for any standards of morality and decency abound, Christianity should promote a holy life. In a world where hurry and haste lead to high levels of stress, Christians under the lordship of Christ can find joy and rest in the Sabbath. They should demonstrate in their lives both the saving power and the lordship of Jesus.

Conviction #3: God restores in believers the wholeness of life in Christ.

Christians do not go to heaven as disembodied souls. The Second Coming restores all of life. Christians should prepare for the Second Coming as whole people. God wants to restore us as whole people. Salvation involves every part of life and being. Jesus wants us to live full and complete lives. In John 10:10 He says, "I have come that they may have life, and have it to the full."

Before Adventism most Christians believed that religion dealt with the soul or spirit of people. At death the soul went to either heaven or hell (or maybe purgatory). The body had little or no meaning. This led to the neglect of health rules and other parts of human existence.

Adventists believe that human beings are a unit. There is not a separate soul which exists by itself. All parts of life affect all other parts. A healthy body and mind help make for a healthy spiritual life, and vice versa. Not only is physical health and mental health a part of religion, so are human relationships. The salvation or healing Jesus wants to give affects all parts of us. For this reason we

- Promote healthful living, including hygiene; abstinence from smoking, alcohol, and drugs; vegetarianism as an ideal; health education; exercise, and proper rest.

- Endorse Christian education.
- Encourage proper social relationships.
- Oppose war.
- Try to care for the physical, spiritual, and mental needs of people in our mission work.
- Believe that when we die, we sleep, waiting to be resurrected as a whole person when Jesus comes again.
- Encourage practical, vocational work as a part of education.

Our Mission Today

More than ever a world that is sick, addicted, and living in ignorance needs the message of a Jesus who cares for and ministers to all parts of our life. A dying world needs the hope of new life lived to its fullness by God's grace and power.

Does It Make Sense to You?

All of these beliefs point to a fuller presentation of Jesus. I am an Adventist because to me Adventism is the fullest presentation of Jesus—

- A Jesus whom I will see again when He comes.
- A Jesus who is Savior and Lord, and who cares enough to guide my life.
- A Jesus who can and does heal not just my soul or spiritual nature, but wants to heal and minister to all I am.

Adventists often feel weird or strange among other Christians for things like the Sabbath, our diet, and standards. We should not forget that things which make us strange to other Christians are often the things that make sense to millions of non-Christians. Adventism often makes more sense to the non-Christian religions of the world than to other types of Christianity.

- Muslims like our high standards in relationship to recreation, modesty, unclean meats, and alcohol.
- Jews identify with us on the Sabbath and some aspects of diet.
- Millions of Buddhists and Hindus teach vegetarianism as an ideal and agree with our stand on noncombatancy and war.

These people are our real mission field! They need to hear about Christ from people they can readily identify with in other areas.

Your Turn

1. Do you really believe that Jesus is the unique Son of God who offers a wonderful salvation which is a free gift? Has it made a difference in your life? How? If you really believe it, what should happen? How would it affect your mission?

2. Do you agree with the unique Adventist emphasis presented here? What parts mean the most to you? What parts mean the least? Why? What do you think are the most important parts of the chapter?

3. Do you believe Adventism is a fuller presentation of Jesus? Why? What could you add to this? How has your faith added to your picture of Jesus? Have we as a church always presented our unique message as it relates to Jesus? What can we do to improve in this area?

Chapter 5

It's Your Church!

While traveling by plane in Asia an Adventist missionary began a conversation with his seatmate, who represented another Christian organization. After hearing briefly about the worldwide church organization of the Seventh-day Adventists, the seatmate stated with obvious envy, "If only we could function as a world church, what strength there would be." This reaction is not uncommon among leaders of other Christian churches and organizations. In this chapter we want to see how the Seventh-day Adventist Church is organized to work effectively, how it helps you in your task, and how you can contribute to it.

 **Think About It**

- What do you know about the worldwide organization of the Adventist church?
- How can local churches get involved in mission?

A Global Church

When you look at the Adventist church, you are immediately struck by the fact that this is a worldwide church. Instead of being organized in national churches that are independent of each other, Adventists have chosen to stay in a global fellowship of churches that are bound to each other by a common faith and a strong organizational structure. From a handful of people in 1863, the church has developed into a truly worldwide movement of over 20 million people. This amazing growth is supported by a church organization both complex and simple at the same time. The complexity comes from the multifaceted work carried on around the world. It involves some 151,000 churches and "companies" and thousands of institutions engaged in an incredible diversity of services and ministry.

Institutions

Best known are perhaps Adventist healthcare facilities, the church's educational work, and the ministry of the Adventist Development and Relief Agency (ADRA). The network of more than 7,800 schools operated around the globe is one of the largest church-operated school systems in the world. Add to that orphanages and nursing homes, over 60 publishing houses, 22 food industries, and countless other projects, and you have indeed an incredibly complex organization.

Departments

Of course, there is also the full spectrum of departmental services. These include Sabbath school, personal ministries, youth, children, stewardship, publishing, health/temperance, family, and women's ministries, which gives support in specialty areas for more successful nurture and outreach.

A Simple Structure

At the same time, the Adventist church is structured in a simple way. There are only one or two organizational levels between the local church and the global organization. The local church is a "family" of Adventist members in a local area who have been granted status as a local church. These local churches are organized either into a conference or union of churches. The conferences are organized into a union covering a larger geographical area.

The General Conference (GC) has its headquarters in Silver Spring, Maryland, and is represented around the world through its "divisions." As of December 30, 2016, there were 84,207 churches organized in 655 conferences or missions, and 135 unions, union missions, or unions of churches. These encompass established work in 215 countries within the 13 divisions and two attached fields of the General Conference. The division/attached fields and their office locations at time of publication are as follows:

- East-Central Africa (ECD), Nairobi, Kenya
- Inter-European (EUD), Berne, Switzerland
- Euro-Asia (ESD), Moscow, Russia
- Inter-American (IAD), Miami, FL, United States of America
- North American (NAD), Silver Spring, MD, United States of America
- Northern Asia-Pacific (NSD), Koyang City, Korea
- South American (SAD), Brasilia, Brazil
- South Pacific (SPD), Wahroonga, Australia
- Southern Africa-Indian Ocean (SID), Pretoria, South Africa
- Southern Asia (SUD), Hosur, India
- Southern Asia-Pacific (SSD), Silang, Philippines
- Trans-European (TED), St. Albans, England
- West-Central Africa (WAD), Abidjan, Cote d'Ivoire

The two attached fields are:

- Middle East North Aftrica Union, Beirut, Lebanon
- Israel Field, Jerusalem, Israel

Support for Mission

But what is the value of this organization that guides the work of the Adventist church around the world? There actually are many values.

Facing Global Challenges

The first value of an efficient organizational structure is the church's ability to address global challenges. Despite all efforts in the past, the mission of the Adventist church is far from finished. Chapter one showed that many millions have never heard the name of Christ. Hundreds of people groups are still completely untouched by the Christian message. Hundreds more have not yet been entered with the Adventist message of Christ's soon return. This challenge demands the mobilization of resources that go far beyond local capacities alone.

Strategizing for World Evangelization

In 1990 the Adventist church created a "think tank" to develop and implement the church's efforts to evangelize the thousands of unreached people groups. This initiative, called Global Mission, has resulted in the mobilization of thousands of Global Mission Pioneers penetrating many new areas and planting thousands of new churches. In addition, this new vision has influenced churches and organizations at the local levels to take the challenge of unreached population groups in the world seriously and find ways to reach out to them.

Coordinating the Worldwide Enterprise

The General Conference Secretariat is responsible for coordinating the global missionary flow of the church. The members of the Secretariat all have specific responsibilities for calling and sending missionaries and volunteers to specific areas of the world. While the number of career missionaries has not increased during the last few years, the number of short-term missionaries and volunteers has exploded, leading to the establishment of the Adventist Volunteer Center (AVC) at the GC Secretariat, which seeks to encourage the further development of opportunities for involvement, for cross-cultural training, and for local church initiatives for worldwide mission. This manual, *Passport to Mission*, is partly sponsored by AVC, which uses it as a primary training resource.

At the beginning of this new century the church is again establishing voluntary mission service, so common in the pioneer days of the Adventist church, as the defining characteristic of the Seventh-day Adventist lifestyle. The diverse structure of the church has the potential to be a great asset in making this vision a reality again by opening up many opportunities for service and bringing mission back to the local church.

Contact the Secretariat at the General Conference or visit their website (am.adventistmission.org/career-openings) for church mission possibilities. Students in Adventist colleges will want to contact their campus mission office for student missionary opportunities.

Training for Mission (Institute of World Mission)

For more than forty years the church has prepared missionary families for cross-cultural service through pre-departure Mission Institutes. These institutes teach future missionaries not only how to live in another culture, but also how to be effective missionaries. They have proven to be a great help to missionaries. This training is a requirement for all regular GC missionary appointees. Through this book (*Passport to Mission*), online mission preparation classes, and training seminars and retreats, the Institute also helps to train volunteers as well as missionaries serving with supporting ministries.

How You Can Contribute

You understand now how the church is organized to support the worldwide missionary enterprise. You have also seen how all this can help you in your involvement in mission. But the most important question is: How can you contribute to the fulfillment of the mission of the Adventist church?

At Home

Remember that mission does not start with an airplane ticket to an exotic place, but in the heart of a believer. To be a missionary means to recognize we are Christ's representatives called to witness of His goodness. So you can become involved in mission right now. There are also specific things you can do to contribute while "at home."

At the very least, you can get informed about the missionary needs in the world. Start bringing missions back into the program of your local church. Is the mission report interesting? When was the last time the different departments of the church adopted a mission project? Why not adopt a people group? You may even do that yourself as a personal project. Collect information about unreached people groups, then select one you will start praying and becoming an advocate for. There are some excellent resources that might help you at the end of this chapter. Several other things you can do are found in chapter 28.

In the Field

As missionaries, you will be a part of some aspect of our church organization. It is most important that you go with a positive attitude toward those you are working with. In the remainder of the book we will help you understand why it is so important to go with the attitude of a learner. Remember that if you desire to bring about change or make a contribution to the organization you work with, you need to communicate thoroughly. Always work in close harmony with the chairperson of your board or committee.

You will discover in various cultures and church settings outside the homeland that there are many different styles of leadership and various approaches which differ from the ones to which you are accustomed. In many ways the success of your work has much to do with attitudes and relationships.

The church is excited that you are interested in serving as a missionary. It needs your support and involvement. As a member of the global church family, you will hopefully find your niche where your gifts and interests can make a difference.

Your Turn

1. How do you feel about the worldwide organization of the Adventist church? What do you think are the strengths of an efficient global church structure for mission?

2. What kind of ministry would you like to serve in?

3. As you consider becoming a missionary, try to locate former missionaries and interview them about their experience.

Part 1 Resources for Further Study

Brown, L. (2005). *Short-Term Missions: A Team Leader's Handbook.* Lincoln, NE: AdventSource. Step-by-step plans for leading successful short-term mission trips.

Bruinsma, R. (1998). *It's Time to Stop Rehearsing What We Believe and Start Looking at What Difference It Makes.* Nampa, ID: Pacific Press. A delightful little book that underlines how our fundamental beliefs impact real-life issues.

Bush, L., & Pegues, B. (1999). *The Move of the Holy Spirit in the 10/40 Window.* Seattle, WA: YWAM.

Dearborn, T. (2003). *Short-Term Missions Workbook: From Mission Tourists to Global Citizens.* Downers Grove, IL: InterVarsity Press. An eight week course for the spiritual and cross-cultural preparation of short-term mission teams.

Dybdahl, J. (Ed.). (1999). *Adventist Mission in the Twenty-First Century: The Joys and Challenges of Presenting Jesus to a Diverse World.* Hagerstown, MD: Review and Herald. An outstanding Adventist book on mission with contributions from Adventist missiologists and leaders.

Fann, A., & Taylor, G. (2006). *How to Get Ready for Short-Term Missions.* Nashville, TN: Thomas Nelson. The ultimate guide for sponsors, parents, and those who go.

General Conference of Seventh-day Adventists, Ministerial Association. (2005). *Seventh-day Adventists Believe: A Biblical Exposition of the Fundamental Doctrines.* Nampa, ID: Pacific Press. An in-depth explanation of basic Adventist doctrine.

Jenkins, P. (2011). *The Next Christendom: The Coming of Global Christianity* (3rd ed.). Oxford, NY: Oxford University.

Johnstone, P. (2010). *Operation World.* Downers Grove, IL: InterVarsity. A gold mine of mission facts which covers all the countries of the world and includes Seventh-day Adventists.

Johnstone, P. (1998). *The Church Is Bigger Than You Think: Structures and Strategies for the Church in the 21st Century.* Pasadena, CA: William Carey Library.

Knight, G. R. (2000). *A Search for Identity: The Development of Seventh-day Adventist Beliefs.* Hagerstown, MD: Review and Herald.

Livermore, D. A. (2006). *Serving With Eyes Wide Open: Doing Short-Term Missions With Cultural Intelligence.* Grand Rapids, MI: Baker Books.

Sills, M. (2008). *The Missionary Call: Find Your Place in God's Plan for the World.* Chicago, IL: Moody.

Weber, L. J., (Ed.). (2010). *Mission Handbook, U.S. and Canadian Protestant Ministries Overseas* (21st ed.). Wheaton, IL: Evangelism & Missions Information Services.

Stott, D. W., & Wright, J. H. (2015). *Christian Mission in the Modern World* (Rev. ed.). Downers Grove, IL: InterVarsity Press. This new edition of a classic book shows that Christian mission must encompass both social action and evangelism.

2

Getting
Charged Up
for Mission

Chapter 6

So Why Not?

Have you ever gone out to eat and not had enough money to cover the bill? Have you taken your car to get fixed at the garage and returned to find the bill twice what you expected it to be? In both cases you were not really ready for what happened because your expectations were wrong. It wasn't much fun, was it? Getting "caught off guard" is never a pleasant experience!

Many problems in the field develop because of similar reasons. Unrealistic goals and expectations along with faulty motives lie behind many of the difficulties that arise in the field. This chapter is an attempt to lead you to honestly confront your goals and motives so that your mission experience can be profitable to you and the people you go to serve. We will also take a look at what it means to be "called."

Goals

One thing that is really important is that we set realistic goals. Setting goals that are either too high (false expectations) or too low (no expectations) can cause a lot of frustration and disappointment down the road.

 **Think About It**

- What picture is in your mind when you think of your mission service?
- What do you expect to be doing?
- How do you see yourself being received by the people where you are going?
- What are your goals for your mission service? Be honest and be specific! Write down what comes to your mind now.

As you think about setting realistic goals, there are several things you can do to help yourself:

1. Interview and talk to as many people as possible from the area you are going to serve. This could include former missionaries (regular and volunteer) as well as nationals from that country. If possible, you should talk to people who have done the same kind of job you are going to do. What kind of professional goals can you set? Evangelistic goals? Personal enrichment goals? Spiritual growth goals?

2. Read and study all the written materials about your host culture that you can get your hands on—especially realistic stories that deal with life and mission in that place.

3. Be adaptable. Even those who are the best prepared will find surprises. Expect that your goals may have to be adjusted as time goes on. When that happens, adapt and go on. Realize that adaptability is one of the most important virtues of all missionaries.

Motives

Now that you have thought a bit about your goals, let us think a bit about your motives. Motives are very important. In fact, they are the driving force behind most of what we do in life. Examining them and dealing with them honestly are a major factor in our self-understanding and preparation for service.

 **Think About It**

- So what are your motives? Why do you want to be a missionary? Be sure to consider both your religious and non-religious motives for going as a missionary.
- Try to list the three most important motives in both of these categories.

Non-Religious Motives   Religious Motives

Non-Religious Motives

If we are honest, we will admit that all of us have mixed motives. Non-religious motives contribute to the decision to go on a mission. This is not necessarily bad. It is normal human nature.

Non-Religious Motives Many Missionaries Have Had:

- Desire to travel
- Boredom—want some adventure
- A break from school or work
- Curiosity or desire to experience other cultures
- Desire to learn a language
- Career or job considerations
- Family tradition
- Decision or wish of a parent, friend, or spouse
- Recruited/sold on the idea
- Escape from a difficult situation

Religious Motives

In addition to these non-religious reasons, however, the Bible does give some directly religious motives for mission.

Love for Christ—In 2 Corinthians 5:14 Paul says that the love of Christ is what compelled him to go. And when Jesus set His own disciples apart for service, He first called them to Himself (Mark 3:13) after they had come to Him, then He sent them out on their mission. Coming to Christ first and being filled with His love becomes our greatest motive for going out in service.

The need of people—Matthew 9:37, 38 says that "the harvest is plentiful, but the workers are few." In chapter one we saw that this is still true today, because even today over two billion people in the world can only be reached by the gospel if someone is willing to cross cultural boundaries to teach them. At the same time, less than 15 percent of Christian workers focus on this group of people without Christ. The song is right, "People Need the Lord."

The commands of Jesus—"If you love me, keep my commandments," Jesus said in John 15:15. When we hear this, many of us think first of all of the Ten Commandments. That's okay, but are those the only commandments Jesus could have meant? What about the "commandment" to mission in the Great Commission that we studied in chapter three? And what about the "great commandment" to love one another? If we truly love our brothers and sisters around the world, we will want to share the Good News of salvation with them, won't we?

Mission plays a crucial part in saving people—Our going out really does make a difference in people's lives. "Hearing" helps bring people to salvation (Romans 1:14, 15) as well as giving them a "more abundant life" in the here and now (John 10:10). God sometimes saves people without our help, but His basic plan calls for our cooperation.

Call to Mission

All of this leads us to think about the "call" to mission. Sometimes we hear someone say, "I think God is calling me to mission." Or "If God calls me, I'll go." What do we mean by a "call"?

To begin with, we must realize that there is a sense in which every Christian is "called." We are called to service, a service that grows out of our love and gratitude for what God has done for us. This love creates in us a desire to share that joy and good news with others. So, there is a sense in which we can say that all Christians are called to be missionaries—not necessarily cross-cultural missionaries, but servants of the Master, nonetheless. But God does call some to a special cross-cultural ministry. We will look at two different ways in which He calls us.

Some people in history have received a special, miraculous call:

- Samuel heard God's voice calling him when he was just a boy.
- Peter and John heard Jesus say, "Follow me and I will make you fishers of men."
- Paul was stopped by a bright light on the Damascus road and heard Jesus calling him by name to be the apostle to the Gentiles.

Most people in the Bible, however, did not receive a supernatural call like those, but circumstances led them to God's mission:

- Esther happened to be in the right place to save God's people from annihilation.
- David was visiting his brothers when God helped him slay Goliath.
- Barren Sarah followed her husband to an unknown land and became the mother of God's people.
- Daniel was captive in a foreign court where he was entrusted with prophecies for our day.
- John Mark failed in his first missionary endeavor but went on to be the first to author a gospel account.

Most of us are also called by "God's gentle leading." We see God at work in our lives, and through various providential leadings we feel God calling us.

- We realize that our gifts or talents especially fit us to serve in cross-cultural environments.
- We receive information (via books, speakers, etc.) that appeals to our mind as well as our heart and "calls" us to serve.
- Past experiences (encounters with missions or missionaries, special times of commitment) call us to a personal commitment.
- We see God leading our spouse to mission and feel Him calling us to support their service.
- A desire to serve God and His church leads us to accept a call to mission.

All of the above factors can be powerful incentives to mission service. First of all, God calls us to Him, and then in love we respond and go where He sends us. He does not command results, but He does expect faithfulness. The results are in His hands, but the willingness to respond to His call to mission is ours.

Your Turn

1. What are your personal goals and expectations for being a missionary? Make a list and discuss this list with a person you trust.

2. What are your motives for getting involved in mission? Make a list and sort them into religious and non-religious. Ask yourself which are your strongest motives? Underline the strongest ones. Are they strong enough to hold up when you face a crisis?

3. Review how God has led you to sense His call to mission. Are you willing to trust His leadings? Why don't you talk with Him about that in prayer right now.

Chapter 7

AreYou Connected?

The woman at the well] represents the working of a practical faith in Christ. Every true disciple is born into the kingdom of God as a missionary. He [she] who drinks of the living water becomes a fountain of life (White, *The Desire of Ages*, 195).

You are venturing forth as a missionary. The main purpose of your mission is to share Jesus, to be an agent of the kingdom of God, and to extend the lordship of Jesus. No matter what else you do (build, heal, teach, dig, or preach), your identity is to be a missionary. This is not so much an activity as it is an identity. It is not what you do, but who you are. In this chapter we focus on the difference between a nominal (i.e., intellectual, objective, nonparticipatory) relationship with Jesus, and a dynamic (i.e., experiential, subjective, participatory) relationship with Jesus.

Case Study

The interviewer looked deep into the eyes of the young man he was interviewing. The young man had been born and raised in a conservative Christian home and church, yet during his college years he had seriously questioned that faith and subsequently cast his lot with an Eastern faith led by a mystic guru.

"What is it that you find in this new faith that is better than the old one?" he asked.

The young man paused reflectively and then replied, "Religion is like a can of soup. As a Christian, all we ever did was to read the label on the can, analyzing its contents. In my new faith we open the can and eat the soup."

How Does One Open the "Can"?

As a missionary, you will meet people of other religions who have "opened the can." They often practice a religion that is woven into the very fabric of their lives. How do you share Christ with people like this? Why don't you start by thinking about your own experience: When have you gotten past the label and "opened the can to eat"? What are some of the results of this experience?

Here are some practical suggestions to open the "can"—

- Interactive Bible study
- Conversational prayer
- Making yourself accountable to a small group
- Dynamic corporate worship with a stress on reflection as well as on the emotional dimension
- Personal, practical involvement or participation in local mission or other's felt needs
- Sacrificial giving

Being a disciple of Christ and a missionary requires a deep personal relationship with Jesus that results in a high level of personal commitment and loving obedience. Let us look at these two basic ingredients of discipleship for a moment.

Commitment

Socrates taught that the unexamined life is not worth living. The truth is that it is the uncommitted life that is not worth living. Commitment is the first component in the life of a follower of Christ. What is commitment?

- Commitment points to the time we made a conscious decision, "Yes, Jesus. I belong to you. Come into my heart and mind; be Lord of my life."
- It is subsequently remade daily, sometimes hourly.
- It involves a continual partnership with the living Lord.
- It is an open-ended commitment, much like marriage, open to a growing, deepening relationship.

If you have made this decision, pause and renew it. If you have not made this decision, now would be a great time to do so.

Obedience

The second component of discipleship is loving obedience to our living Lord. Obedience does not mean perfection, but a relationship.

> All true obedience comes from the heart. It was heart work with Christ. And if we consent, He will so identify Himself with our thoughts and aims, so to blend our hearts and minds into conformity to His will, that when obeying Him we shall be but carrying out our own impulses (White, *The Desire of Ages*, 668).

Out of this relationship we regularly make daily choices that enhance our relationship with Jesus. We regularly engage in activities and disciplines that make these choices natural (e.g., personal devotions, corporate worship, celebrating the Sabbath, helping and caring for others, giving tithes and offerings).

Commitment Faith

So what does it mean to be a follower of Christ? It means to be a person who is committed to Jesus and grows in an obedient love relationship with Him. This relationship we call commitment faith. It is the basis of everything we do.

Your Turn

1. We have talked about living as a committed Christian. What does this mean for you as a missionary? Reread the Great Commission (Matthew 28:18-20) and think about how Jesus' authority is demonstrated in your life on a regular basis? How has Jesus called you to "go"? When and how have you heard this invitation personally?

2. How do I experience Jesus' continuous presence in my life? What disciplines am I currently using to reinforce my commitment and loving relationship with Jesus?

3. Use the spiritual life rating scale that follows to evaluate your present spiritual condition.

Spiritual Life Rating Scale

Use this spiritual life rating scale to evaluate your present spiritual condition. Circle the appropriate number for each item.

My Relationship With Others	1 = low	high = 10
1. I conduct myself with maturity and humility towards others (Phillippians 2:1-8).	1 2 3 4 5 6 7 8 9 10	
2. Witnessing to others is a way of life to me (2 Timothy 4:1-5).	1 2 3 4 5 6 7 8 9 10	
3. I know my spiritual gifts and use them to serve the church (Romans 12:1-8).	1 2 3 4 5 6 7 8 9 10	
4. I am helping other young Christians in their spiritual growth (2 Timothy 2:1, 2).	1 2 3 4 5 6 7 8 9 10	
5. I am helping others with their physical and financial needs (James 2:14-18).	1 2 3 4 5 6 7 8 9 10	
6. I demonstrate Christian character (Galatians 5:22f).	1 2 3 4 5 6 7 8 9 10	

My Relationship With God	1 = low	high = 10
1. I am a Christian and am fully assured of my salvation in Jesus (1 John 1).	1 2 3 4 5 6 7 8 9 10	
2. I acknowledge Jesus as Lord in my life through word and deed (Philippians 3:7-14).	1 2 3 4 5 6 7 8 9 10	
3. I am experiencing the fullness of the Holy Spirit (Ephesians 5:18-20).	1 2 3 4 5 6 7 8 9 10	
4. I am guided by the Holy Spirit.	1 2 3 4 5 6 7 8 9 10	
5. My convictions about truth and reality are based on the Bible and its teachings.	1 2 3 4 5 6 7 8 9 10	
6. I can articulate a biblically-based philosophy of life.	1 2 3 4 5 6 7 8 9 10	
7. I am able to integrate faith and life.	1 2 3 4 5 6 7 8 9 10	
8. I am experiencing the significance of corporate life and worship.	1 2 3 4 5 6 7 8 9 10	
9. I have a regular quiet time with Jesus.	1 2 3 4 5 6 7 8 9 10	
10. I have experienced answers to prayer.	1 2 3 4 5 6 7 8 9 10	

Adapted from Jonathan Lewis, ed. 1996, *Working Your Way to the Nations: A Guide to Effective Tentmaking,* p. 40. Downers Grove, IL: InterVarsity Press. Used by permission.

Getting to Know Jesus

What I Enjoy Doing

Take out a sheet of paper and make a list of twelve to fifteen things you enjoy doing. Think of different seasons of the year and hours of the day, of group and solo activities. Then do the five steps listed below.

Things I enjoy doing	G	S	P
1. Walking in the woods		X	
2. Inviting some friends over	(X)		
3. Working in the garden			X

Step 1: When you have finished your list draw three vertical columns and mark them G / S / P. Then check (X) in the "G" column for those items best done in a group, check the "S" column for those items best done with a significant person, check the "P" column for those items of which you are really proud, and draw a circle around the most important three items in the list. Say to yourself, "That is me. I like me." Behind any facade, this is really you.

What Jesus Enjoyed Doing

Step 2: Think about the life of Jesus as described in the Gospels and in the book *Desire of Ages*. Make a list of some of the things that Jesus really enjoyed doing and that were important to Him. Then reflect on the questions at the end of the list.

Things Jesus enjoyed doing	G	S	P
1. Talking with the Father		X	
2. Healing people	(X)		
3. Going to weddings		X	

Step 3: When you have finished your list, draw three vertical columns and mark them G / S / P. Then check (X) in the "G" column for those items best done in a group, check the "S" column for those items best done with a significant person, check the "P" column for those items of which He was really proud, and draw a circle around the most important three items in the list.

Step 4: Now compare the lists in worksheet A and B. How many of the items do you have in common with Jesus? Which ones could you do with Him? How many can He share with you? What would sharing these activities have to do with building a relationship with Jesus?

Step 5: Finally, list three steps you can take now to improve your relationship with Jesus. Maybe you should also put down the dates when you want these steps to be completed.

Chapter 8

Could You Use Some Passion?

This handbook deals with many facets of missionary preparation. The most basic qualification for the missionary is knowing God. This is not the same as knowing about God or even doing the work you believe God sent you to do. Knowing God involves an intimate personal relationship with the living God and His Son, Jesus Christ.

The most important thing you can do to prepare for your service is to take the time to seriously think about this relationship. For your own sake and for the sake of your mission, please prayerfully and thoughtfully consider your current walk with God and what you can do to strengthen it.

 **Think About It**

Look at yourself and analyze your spiritual life. Take your own spiritual temperature.

- How much time do you spend in devotional time, e.g., prayer, meditation, Bible study, devotional reading, journaling, etc.?

- Is the time you spend adequate or inadequate? Why?
- What would you like to see happen in this area of your life?

Using the simple chart below, trace your spiritual journey through life with a line showing its ups and downs, highs and lows. Where are you now? What are the reasons for your present condition? Note where your high points are. Why are they where they are?

Your Life Map

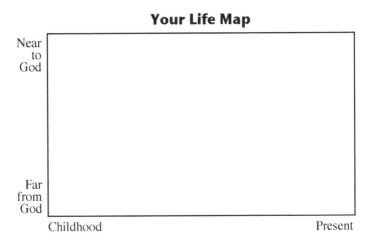

In the pursuit of the spiritual life, we face a number of struggles which fight against our relationship with God.

- Busyness, duties, work, school, and the stress of modern life tend to squeeze out the spiritual.
- The whole lifestyle and educational systems of the contemporary world—too often including Christians and Christian education—have emphasized the material and scientific rather than the spiritual.
- Many of us have a religion which emphasizes facts, doctrines, and abstract philosophical truth rather than the practice of God's presence and practical issues of relationships.

- Many expect mission service to be a benefit to their spiritual life. In some cases it can be, but in others it can put enormous stress on spirituality.
- Many of us will find that those we go to serve have or appear to have a deeper experience of God than we do. That can be depressing!

Principles to Strengthen the Spiritual Life

What can be done in the face of all this? Certain basic principles exist which, if followed, can begin to renew our spiritual life.

Make the spiritual life a priority.

What is most important in your life? What do you do first? Is your spiritual life in that category? If not, why not?

Make a specific time commitment.

Time is the basic stuff of life. What is really a priority for us, we make time for. Scheduling to make time for the spiritual life is an act of obedience and commitment. What specific time of day will you commit to God? Choose a time that fits your temperament. Make sure you give God a time when you are awake!

Live and act as if the spiritual realm is real.

Many fail to pray for themselves or others because they are afraid their faith is weak. Others don't share their faith because they are not too sure about their own relationship with God. Faith comes through exercise. The way to grow and build faith is to simply act as if God will do things. Pray for that person who asks for it. Give God a chance to show what He can do.

Be honest about your life and spiritual condition.

Hiding who you are and your relationship with God never works. You can deceive others and maybe yourself for awhile, but you can never deceive God, and eventually you and others catch on. God has abundant forgiveness and others understand. We can grow if we are honest.

Be willing to risk and experiment.

We're not talking about doing something non-Christian! Some people allow their devotional and religious life to become routine. They never pray, study, or worship in new ways. There are hundreds of appropriate ways to communicate with God, but we often get stuck on a few of them.

Share your spiritual life with others.

Many of us are too private and individualistic in our spiritual life. Christian fellowship is important to spiritual health. We benefit if we share our joys and sorrows, our triumphs and defeats, our hopes and dreams with our Christian friends.

Practices to Strengthen the Spiritual Life

Outside of these basic principles there are specific practices that can be of benefit to our spiritual life. These are suggestions. Don't try to do them all—especially at once! Try various ones as the Holy Spirit leads you.

Become part of a small group for prayer and/or Bible study.

The need for fellowship and mutual caring and encouragement is met best in small groups. Become a member of one if it is available and if it is not, think about starting one. Many different types of materials are available to get you started.

Keep a journal.

A journal is a record of your walk with God and your important experiences. Many people have recently rediscovered the value of journaling and have been helped by it. Especially during your time of mission service you will be helped by keeping a journal of what happens. We all forget more than we realize, and a journal can help you later recapture the highlights of your mission experience. God's blessings and answered prayers are easily remembered if they are written down.

Learn new ways to pray.

One of the best ways to enliven your devotional life is to try new ways to pray. If you are entirely satisfied with what you do now, that is OK, but new horizons can be very helpful. Try praying out loud instead of silently, or prostrate yourself as people did in Bible times. Use a verse of Scripture as your prayer, or pray over the phrases of the Lord's Prayer, using them as your subject. Try conversational prayer with friends.

Try silence, quietness, and meditation.

Many of us are so used to talking to God that we fail to listen to the still small voice. Try being silent before Him or quietly meditating on a verse of Scripture. A reverent listening to God and to our own soul is really a form of prayer.

Try fasting.

In the Bible, prayer is often tied to fasting. Fasting from food is usually meant, but other forms of fasting can be helpful as well. Many of us would benefit by fasting from TV or the radio. Fasting from shopping may benefit others. Fasting for the sake of others is a special form of caring.

Attend worship even if you don't understand the language.

You don't need to understand the spoken language to understand the language of the heart. Listen to the faith and commitment of the people you worship with. Enjoy the presence of God which comes when people worship together. Don't let your differentness keep you from missing a valuable experience.

Use music and art in your religious life.

If certain types of music speak to your soul, bring tapes or music along. Share the music with others. Music that speaks of our relationship with God is a form of prayer. Use it as part of your devotions. If a certain picture or poster speaks to you powerfully of God, take it along as well.

Give generously to others.

Learning to share what you have (money, clothes, time) with others will change you. Give with a joyous spirit and you will be blessed.

Read your Bible and devotional books in a new way.

Read the Bible in a new translation or find a new devotional book. Don't read for speed. It is better to have read one verse thoughtfully and reflectively than two chapters hastily. The Bible is not designed for speed reading. Write a prayer based on a key verse, or memorize a verse and internalize it. This practice truly fixes the Bible in the mind and is more valuable than a ritual reading.

What About You?

How you structure your time with God depends partially on your temperament. It is OK to be yourself. You can find out more about your uniqueness through the Myers-Briggs Temperament Inventory (see the books by Keirsey and Bates and Goldsmith on page 68). Remember that people can eventually tell if you are real or not. People who are genuine before God can be genuine before people as well. A true relationship with God based on time with Him will not only sustain you when the journey gets difficult, but it will communicate to others as well. That is the essence of being a missionary.

Your Turn

1. How do I experience Jesus' continuous presence in my life?
2. What disciplines am I currently using to reinforce my friendship with Jesus?
3. Which of the suggestions given above do you find helpful for your devotional life? Why? Are there other practices that have been of benefit to you? What are they?
4. What would be a realistic, sustainable devotional life plan and schedule for you? Outline it below and commit yourself to following it.

Part 2 Resources for Further Study

Augsburger, D. W. (1996). *Helping People Forgive*. Louisville, KY: Westminster John Knox.

Goldsmith, M. (1998). *Knowing Me, Knowing God: Exploring Your Spirituality With Myers-Briggs*. Nashville, TN: Abingdon.

Hybels, B. (1998). *Too Busy Not to Pray: Slowing Down to Be With God*. Downers Grove, IL: IVP. With instructions for keeping a prayer journal.

Keller, T. (2014). *Prayer: Experiencing Awe and Intimacy With God*. New York: Penguin Books.

Krueger, D. (2013). *Type Talk: The 16 Personality Types That Determine How We Live, Love, and Work*. New York: Random House.

MacDonald, G. (2007). *Ordering Your Private World*. Nashville, TN: Thomas Nelson. Intended to help cultivate the inner life for increasing public effectiveness.

Nouwen, H. (1972). *The Wounded Healer*. Garden City, NY : Doubleday.

Seamands, D. A. (1985). *Healing of Memories*. Wheaton, IL: Victor. How to let God heal emotional wounds.

Warren, R. (2014). *God's Power to Change Your Life*. Grand Rapids, MI: Zondervan.

White, E. G. (1964). *The Desire of Ages*. Mountain View, CA: Pacific Press.

White, E. G. (1980). *Steps to Christ*. Washington, DC: Review and Herald.

Willis, A. T., & Blackaby, H. T. (2002). *On Mission With God: Living God's Purpose for His Glory.* Nashville, TN: Broadman & Holman. By the author of *Experiencing God*, this book focuses on God's call for every Christian to become a part of God's mission.

Yancey, P. (1996). *The Jesus I Never Knew.* Grand Rapids, MI: Zondervan.

Part 3

Dealing with Cultural Differences

Chapter 9

Identify Your Cultural Fingerprint

Most of us remember an experience that made a trip to another country memorable. Often it is some aspect of the new culture we had not yet learned: for example, greeting our foreign host, perhaps being unable to speak the new language, or feeling unsure how to respond properly to the invitation to join the family for dinner. To be an effective missionary we must understand how culture influences every one of us and learn to be sensitive to the ways of our host culture.

 **Think About It**

Have you ever gone to a new place where you were not known? Do you remember what it felt like? Do you remember what it felt like when you first met a person from another cultural or ethnic background? Describe your experience.

What Is "Culture?"

What do you think of when you hear the word "culture?" In everyday language we sometimes use the term "culture" to refer to the behavior of the rich and educated elite. They are cultured because they know how to eat with the proper spoon and fork at a banquet, they know how to dress properly, and they listen to classical music. In the context of studying people, anthropologists have broadened the term "culture" to refer to the way a society lives and thinks.

A Model of Culture

Culture affects all dimensions of our life. To help us think about the different dimensions of culture we will use a simplified model of three circles which are like the layers of an onion. We will see how each layer becomes less conscious but is an extremely important foundation to what is more obvious on the outside.

- *The outer layer*: visible behavior, products, and institutions
- *The deeper layer*: values, beliefs, ideas, and feelings
- *The invisible layer*: worldview

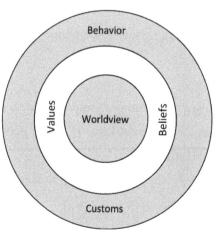

Figure 4. A multi-layer model of culture.

The Visible Layer: Behavior, Products, and Institutions

What is the first thing we notice in another culture? It is people's behavior. People eat, greet each other, sleep, walk, read, and work. We may also observe that there are patterns of behavior. People greet each other in a certain way. All these behavior patterns are learned rather than biologically determined. The products of a people and the institutions of a nation are also part of that outer layer.

Examples:

- In America people shake hands.
- In Mexico and France people embrace.
- In India people may put their hands together and raise them toward their forehead with a slight bow of the head, allowing them to greet many others with a single motion.

The Deeper Layer: Values, Beliefs, Ideas, and Feelings

How can these differences in behavior be explained? They are determined by the values, ideas, and beliefs a society holds about life, the world, and people. These ideas could be likened to inner mental maps that guide people's behavior and actions. Without understanding these more implicit dimensions of culture, many behaviors remain a mystery to the newcomer.

Examples:

- The Indian way of greeting is important in a society where the touch of an untouchable defiles a high-caste person and forces him to take a purification bath.
- Muslims eat only after sundown during Ramadan, the month of religious fasting.

The Level of Assumptions: Worldview

At the deepest level cultures provide answers about what is real.

These answers help people form their views about the questions of meaning and origin, what causes sickness and death. Cultures are not a random accumulation of ideas, behavior patterns, and values, but systems integrated around fundamental assumptions about reality and life.

Each aspect of culture is inseparably linked with other patterns. Even though there are always "loose ends," inconsistencies, and constant change, cultures function wholistically.

How We Learn Culture

To summarize, we can define culture as "the more or less integrated systems of ideas, feelings, and values and their associated patterns of behavior and products shared by a group of people" (Hiebert, *Anthropological Insights for Missionaries*, 30). But you may ask, "If worldview and culture have shaped us so fundamentally, how did we learn culture in the first place?"

Most aspects of culture we learn in early childhood before we know how to reason. We learn everyday things like how to greet; how to dress; what, when, and how to eat; when to go to bed; how to say "no" politely; and how to relate to strangers, friends, and people in authority. Our concepts of family, friendship, relationships, property, privacy, time, and space are developed through parental training and reinforced through social interaction. Rules of proper behavior are reinforced through sanctions. Additional skills we learn in connection with schooling and career training. All these ideas and skills help us to make sense out of life and solve daily problems. In the end we feel that life is "normal" as long as we can integrate what we learn into our cultural frameworks of understanding.

Three Observations

Culture is a total way of life and therefore pervasive. There is no society without culture. Culture is a people's design for living affecting every aspect of life. It functions like colored eye glasses through which we filter what we perceive. We don't really notice the glasses until they get dirty, or until we start using other glasses. Moreover, you can't change one aspect of culture without affecting other parts as well.

Culture makes life meaningful to its people. It provides a society's answers to the basic human questions all people face. These answers give meaning to life and provide an integrated logic to those within the culture even though they may seem strange to outsiders. Culture makes communication possible.

People communicate with each other in various ways. Culture creates the symbol systems (e.g., language, gestures, signs) people need to communicate with each other in an understandable way. Culture is reflected in language. Thus, without knowing the language of a people, missionaries will be limited in their understanding of the new culture.

Implications for Missionaries

What we have learned about culture has many implications for Christian service. Here are some to think about.

Different is not bad. Each culture operates according to its own innate logic. We must be careful not to condemn people whose customs are not like ours as if they deliberately chose a perverted way of life.

Cultures resist change. Since culture embraces all aspects of life, we need to be aware of the fact that we come to a people who already have a set of answers to their questions and a way of life.

The gospel is a change agent. Before we can effectively minister in a new culture, we must first seek to understand it within its own context. Missionaries have often introduced changes without knowing how cultures change.

Change in one aspect affects the whole. When introducing change we must ask ourselves how this change will affect the total life of the people.

Think of a car. You can't change one part without affecting the condition of the whole system.

Scratch where it itches. Because no society is perfectly integrated, Christians may find openings for witness in the problems and questions people cannot answer from within their own culture.

Your Turn

1. In this chapter we developed a basic definition and model of culture. When you think of the three levels of culture, what examples from your own cultural background come to your mind?

    Behavior

    Values & Beliefs

    Worldview

2. Language often reflects the culture and experiences of a people. For example, people living in Michigan are familiar with winter storms and icy street conditions as well as hot summers and ice cream. They use the same word "ice" for frozen streets and ice cream. Eskimos, on the other hand, have many different terms to distinguish between different kinds of ice or frozen conditions. Can you think of other similar examples in your language?

3. Culture is a more or less integrated total design for living in a given society and tends to resist change unless old answers to basic questions are no longer seen as valid. What are some questions in your society which you feel are no longer adequately answered and can therefore become bridges to share Christian answers with people from your culture?

Chapter 10

Conquer Your Cultural Stereotypes

Our culture determines what feels normal, right, and real to us, and what we take for granted. When asked why we sit on chairs instead of on the floor, we may smile at the inquirer's "ignorance" and answer: "That's the way we live here." We assume that this is the way it ought to be! But other cultures have developed other ways to live that may seem strange to outsiders. These cultural differences open the way for cross-cultural misunderstandings, cultural pride, and prejudice to develop.

In this chapter we will focus on ways to deal not only with our conscious difficulties in accepting another culture, but also with those cultural barriers that are rooted in our emotions, beliefs, and worldview.

Case Study

An American girl cleaned the room while her Thai roommate was having breakfast in the dormitory dining hall. When the roommate returned, she became upset, cried, and left the room. Later it became clear that the American girl had placed the Thai girl's skirt on the pillow portion of the bed. In Thai culture, the head is sacred and putting a piece of clothing associated with a lesser part of the body on a place reserved for the head was one of the worst possible insults. Friends and advisors tried to explain to the Thai girl that the American girl's intentions were only good, but the involuntary reaction was so deep that she refused to room with the American girl again.

From Sikkema, M. & Niyekawa, A. (1987). *Design for Cross-Cultural Learning*. Yarmouth, ME: Intercultural Press.

 **Think About It**

If you were the American roommate, how would you feel at this moment? Have you ever been in a similar situation where you offended someone unintentionally? How did you deal with that situation? Describe some of your feelings and thoughts?

God has made human beings so creative that there is an almost infinite variety of patterns of human living. Each culture has developed its own set of characteristics that gives its society distinctiveness and unity. To learn to appreciate this diversity we must become bicultural. There are frequently some obstacles on the way to this goal.

Ethnocentrism

Most of us have grown up in a one-culture setting, hardly aware of the differences in habits and customs within our own culture. The way we do things at home or our group is normal to us. People who differ in accent and habits strike us as "strange." When we confront another culture, our normal emotional response is ethnocentric: we react to other people's "odd" customs through our own colored glasses. Curiously enough this reaction is a two-way street because they also have certain stereotypes of us.

Stereotypes Westerners Have of Non-westerners

They are	But also
Innocent	Interdependent with family and society
Lazy and corrupt	Living in harmony with life
Inefficient	Very spiritual
Emotional	Content
Slow	Have servant attitude
Indifferent	
Poor and uneducated	
Needing help	
Controlled by customs	

Stereotypes Non-westerners Have of Westerners

They are	But also
Aggressive	Educated
Harshly pragmatic	Reliable
Tense	Strong individuals
Discontented	Have secured better lives
Lonely	Free of superstition
Corrupt	Confident
Wealthy and materialistic	Organized
Dominating	
Loud and obnoxious	
Competitive	
Selfish and self-centered	
Have an attitude of superiority	
Preoccupied with efficiency	

Stereotypes may have their value as quick orientation points to facilitate understanding. But since nobody embodies all the characteristics of a particular list, they soon become barriers to understanding. Missionaries must learn to develop empathy and an appreciation of the host culture and its ways. This approach leads us to remember our common humanity before God.

Cultural Misunderstandings

Another barrier to communication is cultural misunderstanding. When we cross cultural boundaries, especially as tourists, we often assume that the symbols and behaviors we find in another culture mean the same as in our own culture. This is a common mistake. What we have to realize is that behaviors are linked to values, beliefs, and worldview assumptions that may differ dramatically from our own.

For example, in North America it is rather impolite to be more than a few minutes late. After letting your partner wait for more than five to ten minutes, you better have some good excuses for being late. Being late thirty minutes is basically inexcusable and rude. But in certain Arab cultures only servants are "on time." Those of higher rank arrive some thirty minutes late after the servants have prepared everything for the meeting.

Values and Culture

In all we do we are guided by our values. However, individuals and cultures differ on what they value as most important. Moreover, as Christians, we also listen to the Word of God. In order to understand cultural differences, we need to distinguish between the different types of values we hold:

- *Personal Values*—These are values that reflect our personal preferences and include such things as cleanliness, security, health, and job satisfaction.

- *Cultural Values*—This category includes values that are top priorities in our dominant (home) culture. Individualism, material success, and independence are examples of top cultural values in the western world. Many non-western cultures place more value on community, cultural heritage, and dependence.

- *Biblical (Eternal) Values*—Obviously, this is the most important area of values we live by. It includes mercy, justice, and love.

As you move to another culture you will discover that the most difficult adjustments will be when your values clash with your host culture's values. If you are unaware of the meaning of cultural expectations, you will find yourself quickly frustrated. Learn to be sensitive to cultural clues.

Be a Learner

So how can you avoid cultural blunders and embarrassments to your hosts? Here are a few tips to help you not judge prematurely from your own cultural perspective as you are becoming a bicultural person.

Become a learner with a servant's heart—It is impossible to become a bicultural person without going through a period of learning. If you want to come close to people, you must approach the new culture as a learner and servant, not as a teacher who judges other's ways before having learned to understand and appreciate them.

Plunge right in—The key to learning a new culture is the attitude we bring to the new situation. Experienced missionaries and anthropologists recommend that we plunge into culture learning right from the start. Venturing into the unknown can be frightening. But soon we see that the risk pays off. People respond with eagerness to help us in our often simple efforts to learn their ways.

Don't assume you know—Be aware of the difference between a passive and active understanding of culture. Many mistakenly consider themselves competent in communicating with "foreigners." They may have studied some of the literature, history, or art of the host culture, met foreign representatives at school or professional meetings, or traveled to foreign countries. But this feeling is deceptive because it is based on the passive understanding of another culture, which does not guarantee that a person will be able to interact effectively with persons of other cultures on their own home ground. To become an effective missionary, you need to develop an active understanding of culture.

Real Learning—Active understanding of a culture involves not only intellectual and rational, but also emotional, aspects. We may accept something rationally, but reject it on an emotional level (like the girl in our case study). Active understanding often comes as we see the limitations of our own cultural background. This is one of the positive aspects of culture shock, which we will deal with in the next chapter.

So What!?

The goal of becoming a bicultural person is to enable you to identify with your hosts and truly appreciate their culture on three levels.

Reasoning and Rational Thinking (Cognitive Level)—Remember, each culture has found its own way of approaching life and its problems. Learn to acknowledge different perceptions of reality and different ways of doing something. There are other ways to build a house than the typical western air-conditioned two-story structure. How disease is caused may be explained differently than by using the germ theory. Some of these explanations may be rooted in folk sciences and religious beliefs. Some may be more adequate than others. But remember that you are not only dealing with a behavior, a way of doing things, or a single belief but with a whole worldview.

Feelings and Tastes (Affective Level)—The fact is that many things are a matter of preference and taste, rather than right or wrong, for example, how you like certain kinds and combinations of food.

Judging and Decision-Making (Evaluative Level)—When you deal with another culture's norms and values, be cautious not to condemn what you cannot understand as an outsider. When evaluating aspects of culture or counseling fellow believers, differentiate between—

- Good and worthwhile aspects to be encouraged
- Neutral aspects to be retained
- Bad or evil aspects and practices which must be dealt with and changed

In most cultures the good and neutral aspects by far outnumber the evil aspects. Thus cultures reflect God's great gift of creativity to humanity.

Rewards

What are the rewards of being a bicultural person? Here are three important considerations to keep in mind when you work through the process of becoming a bicultural person.

- *Identification*—As you strive to learn from other cultures, you will be challenged to overcome your natural tendency towards ethnocentrism and become more effective in ministry to the people as you identify with them.
- *Enrichment*—Becoming aware of other creative approaches to life that are as valid as your own cultural ways will be enriching.
- *Perspective*—You will better understand your own worldview because you have a unique chance to compare and contrast it with others.

Most missionaries will confirm that becoming a bicultural person may not be easy, but it is worth it.

Your Turn

1. Take a look at the list of stereotypes westerners and non-westerners have of each other. Do you hold any of them? Do you think any of them are valid? Why? How might these stereotypes become stumbling blocks for effective cross-cultural ministry?

2. Take a look at the opposite list. Do any of these characteristics apply to you? How do you feel about the way you might be stereotyped by the people of your host culture?

3. As you move to your new ministry, what are some ways you could get involved in the new culture?

4. Think about yourself and your personal and cultural values. What are the top five in each category? How do your personal or cultural values reflect biblical values?

Chapter 11

Prepare for Culture Shock

Would you try running an iOS app (iPhone app) on an Android smartphone? This illustrates what people experience who have been enculturated ("programmed") in one cultural setting (our "operating system") and find themselves uncomfortable and disoriented in another cultural environment.

 **Think About It**

In this chapter we will focus on culture shock—a psychological upset that stems from unfamiliar cues and unmet expectations in a new culture. Can you think of some of the symptoms of culture shock that you already recognize from previous experiences or from your reading?

Why Do We Experience Culture Shock?

Our culture determines what feels normal, right, and real to us. When we go into a new culture, we are trying to process new experiences through our original cultural system which has not yet learned how to read the new cultural clues. Behaviors have different meanings.

Take a basic thing like eating, for example. Besides personal taste, cultural values guide our decisions on what, how, and when to eat, and with what instruments. To us the new foods we encounter may look, taste, and smell strange. In addition, there are new customs and often also a new language. Given the many new and unknown factors you are experiencing, it is easy to feel frustrated, out of place, and ill equipped to deal even with seemingly simple situations. The resulting condition is culture shock, a temporary condition of stress and disorientation a person experiences on the way to becoming bicultural.

Causes

Some of the causes for the experience of culture shock are:

- Inability to communicate
- Changes in routine
- Changes in relationships
- Loss of understanding
- Emotional disorientation
- Disorientation of values

The severity of culture shock depends upon several factors such as your personality, the extent of the differences between the cultures, and the way you deal with new situations.

Symptoms

Some of the more common symptoms include the following:

- Irritation over the local way of life
- Homesickness
- Boredom and loneliness
- Overall feeling of dissatisfaction
- Rising stress, distrust, and depression
- Physical illness, especially chronic headaches, hypertension
- Overconcern with one's health

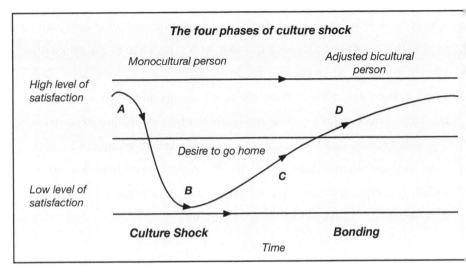

Figure 5. A Model of Culture Shock.

The four phases show that culture shock usually is a process of adapting to stress caused by an unfamiliar cultural environment.

Four Phases

During the process of becoming a bicultural person most people go through four phases.

Initial High (A)—During this phase you usually feel excited, maybe a bit fearful about being in a new country. Your level of satisfaction is high. You are finally there! It's the honeymoon phase of your missionary stay.

Frustration (B)—Sooner or later it hits you. You are here to stay. The different tastes and sounds will not go away. Some of these strange things begin to get to you. You can't seem to understand anybody. Misunderstandings seem frequent now. Your patience is wearing thin. The satisfaction level is low. You feel like going home.

Recovery (C)—The good news is that culture shock is temporary. Your efforts to make friends are crucial and pay off. You begin to laugh again. Some of "their" strange ways begin to make sense when viewed from their viewpoint. Bonding begins to occur.

Acceptance (D)—You begin to feel comfortable again. There is a sense of satisfaction about your work. You are accepting the local climate, food, dress, and customs. You function without anxiety. You make friends and enjoy them. Eventually, you will miss them!

"Danger Zones"

Life in a different culture appears full of potential for cross-cultural misunderstandings and stress. Some "danger zones" are:

- Interpersonal relationships (e.g., how to relate to co-workers, people in authority, or a seller at the local market)
- Cultural incompatibilities (e.g., chickens or other animals in the church)
- Rules of politeness, etiquette, and friendship (e.g., how to say "No" to a request where such a behavior would be seen as very rude)
- Privacy or the lack of it (That's a hard one for westerners!)
- Use of time (Does anyone here wear a watch?) and space
- Communication (Why don't they get it?)

Concerns about climate, food, living conditions, and hygiene are often high on the initial anxiety list. These are usually not the most problematic areas of trouble because we do adjust to different climates quite readily and we can learn to eat new food. The list for cultural blunders, however, seems endless. But don't despair. As you bond with the people of your host culture, you will become more familiar with the cultural clues. Soon you will develop a new sense of security and belonging.

Practical Tips

Here are a few tips to help you deal more effectively with the stress of culture shock.

- *Don't deny but recognize culture shock.* Those who feel they are immune to it may get it even worse. If you bottle up your feelings or act as if you are not affected, you will only isolate yourself.
- *Know yourself.* Learn to strengthen your emotional security through self-acceptance. God made you special with your gifts and talents.
- *Set goals that are realistic.*
- *Seek a reasonable amount of escape*: reading, your favorite music, or a hobby. You may even pack a few books of healthy humor. Humor is often culture-specific. A good laugh may help you across some difficult moments. Make sure you plan for vacation time if your mission is for a year or more. Ask friends for gift subscriptions to your favorite magazines. In any case, allow time for weekly relaxation and recreation.
- *Get to know your host culture.* Try to appreciate unfamiliar ways of doing things as other ways to deal with life's problems and joys, even though different from your own.
- *Improve communication.* Study the language and observe nonverbal forms of communication.
- *Don't isolate yourself.* Remember that culture shock is only temporary and will pass as you learn to bond with people and appreciate the host culture's ways to cope with life and its challenges.

Record your observations and reflections in your field journal. (It is best to start one even before you leave home.) It will provide you with a wealth of insight when you are debriefing with friends, other missionaries, and people back home.

Transition

Transition is an integral part of our life. Some transitions are developmental—a part of normal growth patterns. Some transitions are thrust upon us by circumstance—societal change or personal loss. Other transitions we choose—marriage, education, or career moves. Moving and living internationally intensifies normal transitions and increases the frequency and number of adjustments required. Every transition involves several stages. Each of the stages of transition is a normal, and necessary, part of the cross-cultural adjustment process. Some have proposed that there are as many as ten stages, but let's consider the five stages suggested by David Pollock of Interaction International.

Stage 1: Engagement

We have a sense of belonging and security, position and reputation, friends and responsibilities. We are engaged and committed to our lives and community.

Stage 2: Leaving

A sense of disengagement begins, often subconsciously, leading to a relinquishing of our roles and a loosening of ties. The feelings of withdrawal, exclusion, even rejection can lead to criticism, conflict, and sadness. During this stage reconciliation of relationships needs to occur and proper good-byes said.

Stage 3: Transition

Feelings of chaos, grief, and inner disorientation are at the heart of the transition process. Problems are exaggerated, normal routines disrupted, misunderstandings and ambiguities abundant. Grief and self-centered behavior result. Realistic expectations, an understanding of the transition process, and appropriate self-care can ease the frustration and anxiety.

Stage 4: Entering

As we observe and learn about our new culture, we make mistakes and feel marginal and vulnerable. Our feelings are easily hurt, and ambivalence and fear make even simple actions feel risky. A trustworthy mentor can lessen uncertainty and help us begin to feel tentative acceptance.

Stage 5: Re-engagement

Developing a sense of belonging in a new community requires a willingness to reach out to people, an acceptance of differences in people and situations, a commitment to participation and involvement. The support of others who have made cross-cultural transitions is helpful during this time.

Adapted from D. C. Pollock, & R. E. Van Reken, R. E., 2001. *Third Culture Kids: The Experience of Growing Up Among Worlds,* pp. 199-213. Boston, MA: Nicholas Brealey.

Your Turn

1. The process of adaptation is similar to other experiences of change or transition you might have had, for example, moving to another city, moving into a different house, changing schools, or losing a friend. Recall a transition experience in your life, and describe how you adjusted to it? What were the major challenges you experienced? What helped you to cope with it?

2. How are you preparing yourself for culture shock? List some of the things you plan to do when you will face culture stress. What are a few items you will pack to create your own new sense of "home"?

Chapter 12

Communicate Across Cultural Barriers

"Why is this American so disrespectful when he prays to God? How can he be a spiritual person if he does that?" whispered the distressed-looking woman to her pastor. During prayer the overseas guest preacher, instead of folding his hands, had put one hand to his chin, the other into one of his pockets and played with some loose coins. The impact of the message had been severely diminished by an unconscious gesture interpreted as irreverence in a culture where God is viewed as a sovereign ruler and prayer is considered an act of approaching a holy God.

Communication is the main missionary task. If you are not effective in your communication, your overall effectiveness is hampered. The basic model of cross-cultural communication in this chapter will help you to be better prepared for the task of sharing the gospel in different cultural settings.

 **Think About It**

How do you express reverence in your culture? Have you observed how people of other cultures express reverence? Have you ever noticed that an inoffensive behavior in one culture can be quite repulsive in another?

What Do You Mean?

Communication is the sharing of the same meaning with another person. When you are in a cross-cultural context, it is at first often difficult to understand the meanings that seem to be taken for granted. Meanings can be attached to any form such as a behavior pattern, a word, or product. For example, the behavior of shaking your head can mean approval or disapproval. It is your culture which determines what the different kinds of shaking your head mean. In India people shake their heads approvingly in a way that can be misunderstood by westerners as disapproval.

Communication is a process of sending and receiving meanings on different levels. They can be identified conceptually to help us understand the complexity of the communication process.

- *Cognitive level*—words and concepts and their explicit meaning
- *Affective level*—the feelings and relationships present in the process
- *Evaluative level*—the largely unconscious critical dimension

In real life these three levels affect the communication process wholistically. Thus, ineffectiveness in one dimension may impact the total process.

The Cognitive Level

In western societies this level of communication is clearly of major importance. At this level we communicate words, explicit ideas, and concepts. But other cultures focus more attention on the context of the communication. Anthropologists distinguish therefore between low context cultures and high context cultures. This distinction may be quite helpful.

- Low context people pay attention to words, ideas, and concepts. They may remember the topic of a conversation, but not the names of the people who participated in the discussion. They focus on explicit words rather than on the implicit tone of voice. They enjoy analyzing and comparing ideas. And they prefer a signed contract to a handshake.
- High context people pay special attention to the concrete world

around them. They notice subtle cues in the physical setting of a conversation which communicate important information: sounds, smells, expressions on people's faces, the body language, and the atmosphere of the room. They tend to remember names and details about events. They welcome efforts to learn the local language as a sign of friendship.

The Affective Level

People's notions of beauty, style, and aesthetics influence their tastes and relationships. Missionaries must be sensitive to other people's feelings. There is no communication without identification. Even if you use the right words in a foreign language, people still want to feel you identify with them, share their feelings, and empathize with them as persons. In cross-cultural settings over 50 percent of all communication takes place on this level. You may not be able to speak their language very well. But by attempting to learn it you are communicating that you care about them.

The Evaluative Level

Cultures provide people with standards to make judgments, determining truth and error, likes and dislikes, and right and wrong. We always evaluate what we see, hear, and experience in terms of our own culture. When the messenger does not fit within the established standards, he/she is often perceived as untrustworthy and the message may be rejected.

Example: Western missionaries are often quick to judge what they perceive to be a lack of morality and values in other cultures. However, it may come as a surprise to them that they are judged by their hosts as immoral. Hiebert (1985) reports that people in India considered the dress of missionary women immoral. In their society, the sexiest parts of a woman's body are the calves of her legs. To be dressed properly women wear ankle-length saris. The missionary women wore knee-length skirts.

Form and Meaning

We are often not aware of the meanings behind customs and observable forms that greatly influence the affective and evaluative level of communication. We shake someone's hand to mean hello. In some circumstances it is appropriate to greet a person with a kiss. The custom of Sirano men (South America) of greeting by spitting on each other's chest would easily be misunderstood in western settings as an insult.

The association of a specific meaning (e.g., greeting), emotion (e.g., anger), or value with a certain form (e.g., behavior, product, sign) is called a symbol. The fact that people share a common set of symbols makes communication possible. Since these associations are culturally determined, cross-cultural communication is often difficult. Moreover, symbols not only have "plain" but also "connotative" meanings. Plain meanings of words are relatively easy to learn. Connotative meanings are often hard to discover and a fertile source of misunderstandings.

- *Plain meanings* point to certain things or events, and not to others of a different domain. "Red" means a certain color and not the color black.
- *Connotative meanings* come from different domains. "Red army," and "to be in the red" no longer refer to the color red, but have political or economic meanings.

So What!?

Culture has important implications for the sharing of the gospel. Missionaries need to approach a situation with the hearer or receiver in mind. The important element of communication is not simply the message delivered, but the message the recipient hears.

The Communication Process

Here is a simplified model to summarize several of the concepts discussed in this chapter.

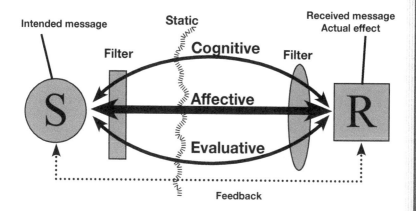

S=**Sender**–Initiates communication by sending a message. To send the message he must encode the message and select a form or medium that will allow him to transmit the intended message and that is understood by the receiver.

R=**Receiver**–Receives, decodes, interprets, and responds to the message. He is limited to receiving the messages in languages and symbol systems with which he is familiar.

Levels of communication–The cognitive, affective, and evaluative dimensions are present in the communication process in various ways.

Medium–The medium is not the message but the symbolic encoding system by which a message is conveyed.

Feedback–Response of the receiver fed back to the sender by various channels and evaluated for the continuing communication process. The importance of feedback can be demonstrated from the telephone experience. In a telephone conversation we depend on some kind of acknowledgment from the receiver that he is listening, since there is no facial contact which we can interpret.

Static–"Noise" factors in the environment which hinder effective communication.

Filters–Factors that influence communication on many different levels of the sender and receiver, e.g., current emotional state, personality, education, values, religion, socio-economic conditions, language factors, and culture. Unless we are aware of the cultural system of other people and sensitive to their values, communication is virtually impossible.

People's feelings are influenced by their level of trust in the messenger. If the communicator lacks credibility in the eyes of the receivers, the message is often rejected. If they sense the missionary's sincerity and love, they are more open to the message.

Conversion involves not only changes in knowledge and feelings but the deepest decisions that people make, affecting their relationships and behavior. People evaluate how their decisions will affect their social support systems. If there is no support from social peers, the pressures of their community may be too great.

Moreover, symbols also reflect the worldview of people, the implicit and hidden assumptions they make about reality. Words for "God," "good," "evil," "salvation," and "sin" often have hidden meanings that are hard to discover because they are taken for granted and not talked about.

Your Turn

1. *Images of Mission* (Hagerstown, MD: Review and Herald, 1995) is an impressive pictorial record of the diversity of the Seventh-day Adventist church around the world. The pictures often reflect the cultural origin of the person who took them. On page 19 of the book, there are pictures showing a poster advertising a Revelation Seminar in Shanghai, China—a lonely man in front of a monumental stone wall (the Ten Commandments) in a judgment hall full of angels dressed in white. How do you think Chinese persons feel about such a painting of the last judgment? You may want to find out if you can. How would you paint this picture differently to communicate a culturally sensitive meaning?

2. In North America sexual immorality is seen as an enormous sin. Missionaries from that part of the world tend to stress proper sexual be-

havior. In South Asia, however, a cardinal sin is to lose one's temper. Too often western missionaries are completely unaware of the implications of impatient behavior on the communication process (especially with their hired helpers). How do you feel about this? Do you have a problem in these areas? What will you do about it?

3. Take a look at the model of communication presented in this chapter. Do you agree with it? How would you modify it? How will you use it to become a more effective communicator?

Chapter 13

Manage Conflict

One of the most common experiences in cross-cultural service is conflict. Even when working or traveling with people you know well, misunderstandings happen and can develop into full-fledged conflicts. Add to that cultural differences, and the potential for conflict is even greater. Missionaries need to understand the nature of conflict and appropriate ways to deal with it.

 **Think About It**

- What are some of the ways people react to conflict?
- How do you feel when you are in a conflict situation?
- What is your typical reaction to conflict?

What Is Conflict?

Conflict is the common human experience of managing differences. People disagree or differ in many ways: roles and behaviors, beliefs and expectations, worldview, attitudes, and values. How we tend to react in conflict is partly determined by our personalities. Beyond that, a missionary must be aware of the fact that every group has their own, often unwritten, rules to handle disputes and differences in a culturally appropriate way.

Not all conflicts have the same intensity. There are probably at least four stages or levels of conflict. Can you think of some examples for each of the four levels?

- Level 1: Unrest
- Level 2: Disagreement
- Level 3: Confrontation
- Level 4: Outright Conflict

How We Deal With Conflict

Each one of us has developed a pattern of behavior in interpersonal conflict that reflects our past experiences, our personality, our cultural normas, and our "theology of conflict." These patterns can become so predictable that experts call them styles of conflict management.

Some of these styles are more appropriate in one situation than in another. By understanding your own preferred pattern and how each style tends to impact a situation, you can learn to make more conscious and productive choices.

On the next pages you will find five typical styles of dealing with conflict. Which conflict style do you feel most comfortable with? Least comfortable with?

The following charts were adapted from N. Shawchuck, 1983, *How to Manage Conflict in the Church.* Schaumburg, IL: Spiritual Growth Resources.

1 Avoiding (The Passive Turtle)

Motto
I will stay out of it

Biblical Example
Adam avoiding God after sinning (Genesis 3:9-10)

Intent
- To stay out of conflict
- Be neutral
- Others are responsible for the conflict
- Not my problem
- I don't care
- Sometimes: Conflict-is-wrong attitude

Behavior
- Unassertive and passive
- Does not cooperate in defining the conflict
- Often denial that problem exists
- Withdrawal

Results
- I lose—you lose
- Negative nonproductive strategy
- Abdicating responsibility
- Produces frustration

When Appropriate
- Problems are not your responsibility or without long-term importance
- Participants too fragile and insecure
- Differences are irreconcilable
- Confrontation will not accomplish anything
- Some parents should use this style

Don't Use
- For important issues
- When issues will not disappear but continue to build

---

2 Accommodating (Lovable Teddy Bear)

Motto
I will give in

Biblical Example
Lot and Abraham (Genesis 13:5-9)

Intent
- To preserve relationships at any cost
- Getting along seen as more important than the conflict issues
- Relationships more important than work and goals

Action
- To preserve relationships at any cost
- Assertive regarding the solutions of others but not one's own
- May even be willing to accept the blame for the conflict

Results
- I lose—you win
- Does not resolve conflict
- Winners assume their ways are superior
- Unrealistic
- Ends up a doormat

When Appropriate
- Relatively minor issue
- When one's own ideas are not helpful, and better or several equally good solution are offered
- When long-term relationships are more important than the short-range conflicts

Don't Use
- To evade issue
- When others are willi to deal with the issue

3 Compromising (The Wily Fox)

Motto
I meet you halfway

Biblical Example
Council in Jerusalem (Acts 15:1-35)

Intent
Win a little—lose a little
To partially satisfy all parties
Popular with politicians, collective bargainers, and international negotiators

Action
• Negotiation and bargaining
• We agree to x if you agree to y
• Flexible style
• Uses persuasion if not manipulation

Results
• Both win some and lose some
• May result in ineffective solutions
• Does not engender full commitments to carry solutions out
• May salvage stalemates
• Often achieves the good since the best is not possible

When Appropriate
• When goals of all parties are valid
• Differences are not worth fighting for
• Time doesn't allow for deeper solutions

Don't Use
• To accommodate unrealistic positions or bad solutions
• If commitment is doubted

4 Competing (The Aggressive Shark)

Motto
I will get my way

Biblical Example
Saul's anger toward Jonathan (2 Samuel 20:30-33)

Intent
• To win
• Assumes that there are only two possibilities in conflict: to win and to lose
• Winning is better
• One's own values, goals, ideas are of supreme importance

Action
• Assertiveness, domination if necessary
• Smooth diplomacy to raw power, but with the same goal: to win
• May manipulate
• Message: I know what is best

Results
• I win—you lose
• Creates polarization
• Frustrates the defeated
• Often grows hostile
• Does not work: one may win the battle but not the war

When Appropriate
• Decision must be made very quickly
• For necessary but unpopular decision
• A person's future depends on it

Don't Use
• When destroying others to get one's way
• When loser can't express needs

5 Collaborating (The Wise Owl)

Motto
Let's work together for everyone's good

Biblical Example
Wisdom of open communication (Proverbs 27:5-6)
Not often practiced

Intent
- To achieve a win-win for all parties
- Issues and people are considered important
- Assumes people are able to solve their own problems
- Appreciates the value of each person
- Respects each party's ideas and goals, while also seeking to maintain a good relationship

Action
- Assertive, also flexible
- Commitment to win-win solutions
- Promotes respect, open communication
- Firm yet sensitive to people's feelings
- Ensures fairness
- All parties must be willing to cooperate

Results
- I win—you win
- Creates participation
- Honest clarification of issues/interests
- Shared decision-making and implementation
- Creativity mobilized
- Both parties get what they want, often in a new way

When Appropriate
- In most conflicts
- Especially involving long-term goals and relationships
- Requires maturity and patience
- Should be practiced more often

Don't Use
- When conditions and time are too short
- When commitments are not present
- When abilities are not present

Cultural Differences

Each one of us has a preferred personal conflict management style. But in cross-cultural situations you must also be aware how your host culture approaches conflict management. To know what is appropriate in a given situation, be sensitive to at least these three questions:

- How is conflict dealt with in my host culture?
- How is conflict handled in my own culture?
- What are the biblical principles that can be used to interact with cultural traditions redemptively?

Some factors that influence the way societies handle conflicts are:

- *Social organization*—Who has authority? What are the social roles of those involved? How are decisions made?
- *Power distance*—How much power does a leader have in comparison with other people?
- *Individualism*—How much freedom do individuals have to make their own decisions?
- *Group orientation*—How important is the group?
- *Channels*—Are there appropriate "channels" to resolve conflicts?

How do these factors influence the way conflict, both group or personal, is handled? In individualistic western cultures open criticism and face-to-face confrontation are allowed as ways to resolution. Committees are also used to balance individual freedom. In group-oriented cultures, where "saving face" is an important concern, it may be unacceptable to expose the vulnerability of individuals. Conflicts may be resolved through mediators. Other societies settle conflicts and make decisions by consensus announced only after lengthy periods of informal discussion and consideration. Committees may not work effectively in such contexts.

So What!?

Missionaries are often unaware of their own cultural context in which they have learned how to deal with conflict. Moreover, Christians fail to appreciate that the Bible has been written to people in specific social contexts applying universal kingdom principles for specific social action. The result is that missionaries often choose biblical passages in harmony with the values of their own social environments and apply them in ways which may violate other fundamental biblical values, such as humility, love, and respect for one another: How Matthew 18 is often used is a case in point.

Biblical Principles

In Matthew 18:15-17 Jesus instructed His disciples how to deal with sin in the church. How do westerners approach this text?

- *Private confrontation*—Westerners often understand Jesus' instruction as a command for private, face-to-face, open confrontation.
- *Public confrontation*—If this procedure is not successful, the next step is to follow it up by using authority figures eventually leading to public confrontation.

While there may be times for public confrontation of sin in any culture, the process described reflects an interpretation of Scripture that is derived from western roots. Those who have lived in a group-oriented culture know how inadequate and destructive such an approach can be. But what are the alternatives? When we take a look at the whole chapter as the context for this passage (especially verses 4, 14, 19, 23, and 35) we find that Jesus is stressing qualities like humility, sensitivity, compassion, unity, servanthood, and a forgiving spirit. This is important as we think about applying Christ's instruction in non-confrontation-oriented cultures.

Instead of using Matthew 18:15-17 as a call for confrontation procedures unacceptable in cultures that value group relationships, we can try to use the powerful principles that this text contains. Furthermore, we must make sure we also consider other scriptural instruction on how to deal with conflict.

Be Sensitive

The scope of conflict—Exercise caution and wisdom in situations of conflict by restricting the scope of the disagreement to "just between the two of you." Remember the proverbs that instruct people to exercise caution (Proverbs 3:30; 20:3; 25:8).

The goal of conflict resolution—Restore relationships with those with whom you have disagreements. Jesus affirms the centrality of love in neighborly relationships (Matthew 22:39, cf. Philippians 2:3).

Use the counsel of others—Humbly rely on the counsel of others, rather than on personal judgment. The purpose of having two or three witnesses is to invite counsel as well as support. James 1:19 admonishes to be "slow to anger," and Paul encourages us to patience and unity (Ephesians 4:2-3), and to avoid strife (2 Timothy 2:14; 1 Corinthians 3:3).

The use of mediators—The Bible contains valuable examples of the use of mediators, messengers, gifts, and feasts of peace for restoring peace. See 2 Samuel 3 (Abner and David), 1 Samuel 25 (Abigail, Nabal, and David), 1 and 2 Samuel (Jonathan and Saul).

Implications for Missionaries

As a missionary, you will be more effective when you seek to apply biblical principles in a culturally sensitive way. The following three principles might help you in this endeavor.

1. Understand the social context in which you practice ministry to determine whether direct or indirect modes of decision-making and confrontation are appropriate.

2. When you have understood your environment, examine how you can live a transformed life, employing kingdom principles to engage the people of that society to redemptively deal with conflict and discover the bond of unity and peace.

3. Understand that the social environment of the Book of Acts and the Epistles is characterized by formal confrontation, majority rule, and arbitration of disputes. Distinguish between process and ethical/moral principle. People are saved not through procedures, but through a right relationship with Christ and the transformation that comes through Him.

As you grow more sensitive to cross-cultural factors, you will also become more effective in managing conflict.

Your Turn

1. Review the five styles of handling conflict. Which styles have you used? In what situations? How effective are you in resolving conflicts in your own culture without creating bitterness?

2. Review the ways the principles of Matthew 18 are employed in the resolution of conflict in your own culture. How do you feel about these? Can conflict be approached the same way in your host culture? Why don't you try to discuss this question with someone who knows your host culture well. Then jot down the most important principles you learned.

3. How do you feel about the key principles for cross-cultural conflict management we discussed in this chapter? Write in your own words how you will use these principles in your ministry to be an agent of peace and unity.

Part 3 Resources for Further Study

Cornes, A. (2004). *Culture From the Inside Out: Travel and Meet Yourself.* Yarnouth, ME: Intercultural Press.

Donovan, K. (2002). *Growing Through Stress* (Rev. ed.). Berrien Springs, MI: Institute of World Mission.

Elmer, D. (1993). *Cross-Cultural Conflict: Building Relationships for Effective Ministry.* Downers Grove, IL: InterVarsity Press.

Elmer, D. (2002). *Cross-Cultural Connections: Stepping Out and Fitting In Around the World.* Downers Grove, IL: InterVarsity Press.

Elmer. D. (2009). *Cross-Cultural Servanthood: Serving the World in Christian Humility.* Downers Grove, IL: InterVarsity Press.

Hesselgrave, D. J. (2014). The Role of Culture in Communication. In *Perspectives* (4th ed.) edited by R. D. Winter & S. C. Hawthorne (pp. 425–429). Pasedena, CA: William Carey Press.

Hiebert, P. G. (1985). *Anthropological Insights for Missionaries.* Grand Rapids, MI: Baker.

Lane, P. (2002). *A Beginner's Guide to Crossing Cultures: Making Friends in a Multi-Cultural World.* Downers Grove, IL: InterVarsity Press.

Lingenfelter, S. (1998). *Transforming Culture: A Challenge for Christian Mission* (2nd ed.). Grand Rapids, MI: Baker.

Stewart, E. C. & Bennett, M. (2011). *American Cultural Patterns*. Boston, MA: Nicholas Brealey.

Storti, C. (2001). *The Art of Crossing Cultures* (2nd ed.). Yarmouth, ME: Intercultural Press.

Living in a Different Culture

Chapter 14

The Incarnational Missionary

So, you've made the decision. You're definitely going to be a missionary. Now what? You have a million questions, right? And several thousand concerns (not to mention several thousand more that your mother has). You're excited, of course, but .... You're committed, but what if.... It seems like a great idea, but what about...? Is that how you're feeling right now?

Well, join the club. We've all had questions and doubts and concerns (sometimes called fears). Let's face it—we're going into unknown territory. A new place. New job. New culture. New language. New challenges. We want to succeed. We want to make a difference. We want to be "good missionaries." But how do we go about it? In addition, most of us have heard "horror stories" about missionaries who have gone abroad and been really obnoxious. And we definitely don't want to do that—right?

 **Think About It**

How can we avoid coming across as arrogant and culturally insensitive? How can we live in a new place in such a way that we do not offend, repel, antagonize, and in other ways alienate those whom we are trying to reach? In other words, how can we be successful missionaries who draw people to ourselves, Jesus, and the gospel rather than turning them away?

How God Modeled Incarnational Mission

Let's begin our search for some clues on "how to be a successful missionary" by looking at some significant portraits of God and Jesus (our model missionaries) that are scattered throughout the Bible. From these "snapshots" we can see how they interacted with people who were different, even estranged from them. Then we can ask what their example means to us.

God with Us

At the very beginning of recorded history, before sin even entered, we find an important picture of God. He is walking and talking with Adam and Eve in the Garden of Eden at the close of each day. There they are. Together. Simple though it is, this scenario sets the stage for the thousands of years of interaction between God and humanity that have followed. God has always wanted to be together with His people.

Then when God brought the children of Israel out of Egypt and He wanted to show them clearly that He was there with them still, He stayed right in their midst in the form of a pillar of cloud by day and fire by night. And when He gave them the directions for the building of the tabernacle (and later the temple), He clearly stated that it was for the purpose of living "among them." Together, again.

Last of all we see Jesus, referred to as "Emmanuel" in both Isaiah and Matthew: "God with us." God left behind the glories of heaven, the companionship of angel friends, the food, clothes, language, and culture of heaven, to come to this backward, dirty, degenerate mission field called earth to be with His people again. He lived with them for 33 years—eating their food, wearing their clothes, speaking their language, thinking their thoughts. Together, again.

This is what we call "the incarnation." And this is God's example to us of what real mission is about. It's being with the people we've come to serve. Close. Together. Living as much like them as is possible. We sometimes refer to this as "missionary identification."

How Jesus Identified With Us

What did incarnation mean for Jesus? In 2 Corinthians 8:9 we read, "For you know the grace of our Lord Jesus Christ, that though he was rich, yet for your sakes he became poor, so that you through his poverty might become rich." Just exactly what this meant is outlined very clearly in Philippians 2. First of all, He gave up His status—equality with God and His identity as God. (He still was God, of course, but He did not use His divinity nor was He recognizable as God.) In addition, He gave up His independence and actually became a servant.

He also gave up His immunity to the difficulties of life and became weak and vulnerable. Lastly, He totally identified with the people He came to serve and save. To any observer, Jesus was a first-century Jew living in a tiny underdeveloped country in the Middle East.

The incarnation of Christ helps us to understand something very practical. By following the example of Christ in identifying with people we are in fact saying to the people we are serving—

- Your ways are good and valuable and I respect them.
- I am not superior or better than you.
- I like you and want to understand you better.
- I want to learn from you.

But what does that mean to us today in the nitty-gritty, everyday areas of life?

Attitudes of an Incarnational Missionary

The first (and most important) thing that is affected is our attitude.

- We consider others as our equals, even superiors, accepting the role of a learner.

- We also become a servant, giving up our rights to be "in charge."

- We cast in our lot with those around us, experiencing, as much as possible, life as they do.

- We try to see the world through their eyes, rather than asking them to look through ours.

- We choose to see the good around us, cultivating a sense of tolerance and acceptance.

- We admit that our own culture is less than perfect. We remember that there is no person, no nation, that is perfect in every habit and thought. One must learn of another. Therefore God wants the different nationalities to mingle together, to be one in judgement, one in purpose. Then the union that there is in Christ will be exemplified. (White, *Historical Sketches of SDA Missions*, 136)

Behaviors of an Incarnational Missionary

Second, incarnation or identification affects the way we live from day to day—eating, dressing, housing, shopping, playing, and even worshiping. Though we may never be able to do everything in the same way as those of our host culture, we nevertheless need to make an effort to adapt to as many ways as we can.

Eating

Whether the staple food is rice, noodles, pasta, potatoes, or cornmeal mush, we learn to eat it gracefully, hopefully, even with gusto. We curb our urge to spend most of our salary on imported foods from home that others can only see as an unnecessary luxury—a silent symbol of our separateness.

Dressing

Whenever possible, we try to fit in with whatever the appropriate dress is for the place and position we have been asked to fill. How do teachers (nurses/pastors/government agents) dress? What is considered modest/immodest? What is considered ostentatious? What is considered inappropriate for church? Work? The beach? In other words, how can you dress in such a way that you will blend in the best and not cause offense?

What that means is that if women go swimming in dresses instead of swimming suits and don't wear shorts even for sporting events in the place you are serving, you will want to tuck those items of clothing into the bottom of your drawer and leave them there for your entire stay, just as Jesus tucked His robes of glory away during life on earth. And if men do not wear beards or neckties or bright-colored shirts in the place you are serving, you will follow Jesus' example by getting rid of yours for the duration of your term of service.

Housing

In times past, it was quite customary for foreigners, including missionaries, to live in very nice houses—much nicer that most of the local people could ever afford. As you can imagine, this caused a great deal of ill-will. Fortunately, in many places this is no longer true, though to some extent the tendency has survived. There is, however, still a tendency for us to take our standards of living with us, perhaps subconsciously expecting things to be "just like back home"—tiled bathrooms and kitchens, hot water heaters, spacious rooms, etc. As incarnational missionaries, we will be willing to accept housing that is much simpler and plainer than we would have back home. If single teachers live in a room with a small bathroom attached, and the only furniture is a bed, wardrobe, table, and two stools, we will accept that housing with grace.

Shopping

Most places we serve have a variety of options for shopping. There will probably be local markets, small shops, and in many cases, various types of department stores—ranging from relatively modestly-priced ones that many local people can occasionally shop at, all the way to very exclusive ones that only expatriates and very wealthy local people can afford.

Where would Jesus shop? Whether we like it or not, where we shop does make a statement both about how we use our money and about how much we are trying to identify with the people we have come to serve. Unfortunately, the quality of the products available in some of the local markets and stores may not be quite up to the standard we are accustomed to, and we at times find this frustrating, but we must remember that this is the only choice most local people have and if we are going to be "with them" as Jesus was "with us," we will shop where they shop as much as possible.

Playing

People in every country have their own ways of relaxing and playing together. Part of fitting into a new place and becoming one with the people is learning to enjoy playing with them in every way that is morally acceptable. This frequently calls for some choices and adjustments. We may have to exchange our love of football and learn to play cricket; forego the traditions of our national holidays in exchange for the wonderful festivities of some of the local holidays; set aside our dependence on TV, videos, and movies to experience the fun of community that is at the heart of relaxation in many parts of the world. Playing together with the people we've come to serve—that's the goal.

Worshiping

You may never have thought much about it, but the truth is that worship is actually a very cultural event. That's hard to believe when most of the worship services you've ever attended all looked pretty much alike, but there are really very few "rules" that govern worship practices worldwide. Even a brief tour through the Bible and history will show you that there are many ways that Christians pray, experience music, and show reverence to God. Identifying with the people in worship means that we allow, and even encourage, people to worship God in ways that may be very different from our way, but that are relevant and meaningful to them.

Removing one's shoes before entering a house of worship is an important part of showing respect and reverence in some cultures; chanting may be more meaningful than singing; prostrating oneself in prayer better than standing or kneeling. Just as Jesus worshiped in the synagogues of Israel and followed the other religious practices that had become a part of normal Jewish worship in His day, we also join people in worshiping God in ways that feel appropriate and meaningful to them.

But How!?

In this chapter we have looked at the question of incarnational ministry and what its implications are in the life of a missionary. It sounds good, right? But how do we really do it?

To consider how it is accomplished we have to look at the "other side" of incarnation. We started out by thinking about Jesus—how He became one with the people and thus became our example. Galatians 2:20 points us in the direction of how we can follow in His footsteps. "Christ lives in me. The life I live ... I live by faith in the Son of God, who loved me and gave himself for me." If Christ is living in me, He enables me to become one with the people. John 15:5 further reminds us that only as we are abiding in Christ (the vine and the branches) can we bear any fruit. It is knowing Christ and experiencing His love intimately, having Him "in us" that then compels us to serve as He did (2 Corinthians 5:14). And finally, Paul reminds us that we "can do all things through Christ who strengthens us" (Philippians 4:13). Not I, but Christ—that's the foundation of incarnational mission.

So that's the good news: He who called you will live in you and enable you to live in a way that will build bridges, not barriers.

Your Turn

1. How would you feel about someone who came to live in your country and made absolutely no effort to "fit in"? How would you feel about someone who not only made no effort to fit in, but was almost arrogant about being different and maintained their separateness? How would you feel about someone who made some basic efforts to adjust and adapt to your country? Which one would it be easier to become friends with?

2. Of the areas of identification mentioned, which do you feel will be the easiest for you? Why? Which will be most difficult? Why?

3. What are some practical things you can do to make the difficult ones easier?

Chapter 15

Learning the Language

In the last chapter we talked about the whole concept of incarnation—becoming one with the people we are living with. As we discovered, this type of ministry affects every aspect of our life. But there is one more area that is perhaps the most important of all for a missionary who is seeking to follow Jesus' example: language learning.

 **Think About It**

Can you imagine what it would have been like if Jesus had brought a translator from heaven and preached all His sermons and taught all His lessons through a translator for 33 years? Strange thought, isn't it? Being able to communicate with people in their own language is very much a part of incarnation, of being together with the people.

Reasons for Learning the Language

So, why is it so important for us to learn as much of the language as we can? Here are the most important reasons:

- It is the foundation of identification and bonding.

- It breaks down barriers.

- It increases your efficiency at doing your job.

- It's the only way to truly communicate and reach people's hearts.

- It's the only way to ever really understand the culture and the people.

- It's the only way to really know what's going on.

Myths About Language Learning

Learning a language, however, is easier said than done. Not only is it a challenge, but frequently you will hear a lot of "reasons" given why going to all the trouble to learn the language is not really necessary, or not possible or practical.

- You don't need to study—you'll just "pick it up."

- You really don't need it—most people you'll deal with speak English.

- You can just use a translator—they'll understand him/her better, anyway.

But you guessed right. These reasons soon prove not to be true. Here is why. Very few people just "pick up" a language. Most of us need some help—a proper language school being the best option, but a trained or experienced tutor a few hours a day can also work well. The bottom line is that initially you need to be intentional about learning a language and have someone experienced to guide you.

While it is true that in many places many of the local people speak English (or French or Spanish or whatever) fluently, the reality is that for most of them this is not their mother tongue, and may, in fact, be the language associated with a colonial power. Their "heart language" is still the language they learned at their mother's knee and will always be the most significant language to them. To truly identify with them (plus others who don't speak the second language at all) we need to make an effort to reach them in their "heart language."

It is true that institutions in many places have gifted translators who can be of great help to you. But a translator is always an unconscious barrier between you and the people with whom you are wishing to communicate. To be truly "together with them" you need to be able to speak to them in their first language.

How to Learn a New Language

Since learning the language of the people is so important, how, then, can you go about it? You are probably thinking by this time that this is a pretty unrealistic expectation. You may be planning to serve for only a year or two, so how are you going to learn a language in a short amount of time? Well, it is amazing how much language you can learn in a short amount of time if you really set your mind to it.

To begin with, you need to have a positive attitude—"I think I can ..." (And you really can—honest!) In addition, it helps to really be convinced of the importance of language learning. That will keep you going on rough days! It also helps to be a bit childlike. We set our adult pride aside and become willing to make mistakes and "play" with the language, knowing we won't be perfect at first. This obviously involves being a risk-taker— something that is a must for learning a language. Sooner or later you just have to stick your neck out and say something that very well may create some confusion or laughter at first, but at the same time will earn you the appreciation and respect of the local people, because you are making the effort to become one with them.

Well, there you have it. You can learn a language. You can come closer to people's hearts by speaking to them in their own heart language. You can experience the joys of being able to really communicate in a new language. Go for it!

Tips for Language Learning

Use a native speaker to guide you as a tutor or informant.

Practice "active listening"—really focusing on the sounds you hear swirling around you at first. This naturally involves some serious concentration—listening for sounds and ultimately words. Remember your brain can't help you create the new sounds until it has truly heard them.

Find ways to get "comprehensible input." What does that mean? It means you need to find people who will treat you like a child, speaking "mother-ese" to you—the simplified, repetitive language we speak to children, accompanied with lots of body language to make it comprehensible.

Focus on all aspects of the language—beginning with listening. As an adult, however, you can benefit by learning the writing system early on so that you can get input from reading as well as listening.

Pray for the Lord's blessing on your efforts.

Your Turn

1. How many languages do you already know?

2. How did you learn them?

3. Can you use those same principles to help you learn another language?

Chapter 16

Reality Check

So here you are—almost "on your way." Probably you're planning what and how to pack, looking ahead to the unknown and exciting adventure you're facing. Naturally you have dreams and expectations of what you'll encounter when you get "over there" (wherever that may be), dreams that are based on many things. When we (the authors) were kids we read lots of mission stories and decided early that we wanted to be missionaries. Our dreams of mission began a very long time ago. What about you? When did you begin to develop missionary dreams? Like us, you may have read stories that whetted your appetite for mission. Maybe you listened to missionaries on furlough or student missionaries who came to your home church or schools. Maybe your interest is more recent, stemming from the urging of a friend or the urging of the Holy Spirit in your devotions or in a meeting. No matter where they began, however, now you're getting ready to turn those dreams into reality. Praise the Lord!

Having dreams is valuable, actually indispensable, for a missionary. But dreams have to be balanced by reality or they can end up disappointing— even mocking us—leading to dissatisfaction and ultimate disillusionment.

So, let's take a look at a few areas that we'll face in what we'll call a "reality check."

The Place

Going to a new place, we naturally have certain ideas about what it will be like, how it will look, etc. Without really thinking too much about it, many of us expect all mission fields to look kind of alike—tropical paradises with white sand and palm trees, simple thatch and bamboo houses nestled in an exotic jungle, and of course dugout canoes for transportation. Sound familiar? We may know better, but this mental image lingers on.

The reality is that mission fields come in all sizes and shapes. And in today's world, because the majority of the world's population lives in mega-cities, this of course means that the greatest mission fields are the world's cities. And cities are much the same the world over—big, crowded, dirty, and (by some standards, at least) ugly. They may be tropical and we may see a few palm trees, but somehow cities just don't fit our "mission field" stereotype. The question we have to ask ourselves, then, as we look at reality is: Are cities less of a mission field than jungles? Is a modern suburb full of people who have no knowledge of Jesus less in need of the gospel than an isolated village? The obvious answer is no! But ending up in a sprawling city with its inherent challenges just doesn't initially fit our dream of what a mission field is. The first reality is that a mission field is anywhere that people need to know the Lord—even a city!

Ourselves

A second area to look at is ourselves as "real missionaries." When we were kids the stereotyped "real missionary" was the pith-helmet-clad semi-saint with a tattered picture roll permanently tucked under his or her arm, perpetually hiking through jungles. The reality is that today's missionaries have probably never seen a pith helmet and would laugh at the thought of being semi-saints. Missionaries are ordinary people who happen to be working in cross-cultural settings far from home.

Naturally, most missionaries would aspire to be new, improved versions of their former selves, but unfortunately, becoming a missionary doesn't necessarily make us any different. We will almost certainly have the same basic personality traits—good and bad—we've always had. We'll have similar temptations and struggles, strengths and weaknesses. We don't suddenly become immune to the challenges of life just because we move to a new place as missionaries. The reality is that one of the beauties of God's plan is that He takes us just as we are (flaws and all) and uses us in His service. Oh, He definitely works on us along the way, as we let Him, but we shouldn't be shocked or disillusioned if we find that we are still basically the same person we've always been when we arrive in the mission field, not some super- (or even semi-super) saint. God won't be surprised. Neither should we! That's the second reality.

The Work and People

The third area to consider is the work and the people to which we are called. Again we have those images in our dreams from the past—rows of adoring children hanging on our every word; droves of people welcoming us with open arms; ourselves teaching or baptizing throngs of eager new converts. Of course, such events do still take place in mission today; and we can guarantee you that you will meet and make friends with some of the most wonderful people on earth—people that you will grow to love; people you will miss immensely when you have to leave.

However, your encounters will be somewhat different from that stereotyped image you may have. Much of what missionaries do is in areas where the work has been going for many years and is already well-established. They frequently serve in a supportive role, working in an already-established institution or organization. Unfortunately, you may also inherit some challenges that have grown out of misunderstandings from the past. Remember, the people where you will serve have already had many encounters with foreigners—missionaries and others—before you arrived on the scene. Some of these encounters have been positive. Unfortunately, others have not. The scars left from some of these not-so-positive past encounters frequently cause attitudes of distrust and even dislike for foreigners today. You, therefore, may at times face (or at least sense) caution, distrust, antagonism, and occasionally, outright hatred. In addition, nationalism can at times cause people to have an anti-foreign spirit which may lead to a "Missionary, go home!" attitude.

If something like this should happen, does that mean that you misunderstood your call? Does it mean you should respond in kind? Obviously not! Missionaries can frequently be agents of peace and good will, binding up the wounds from the past and bringing healing to broken relationships.

The Four H's of Reality

Having looked at the realities about our place of service, ourselves, and the work we will do, let's now turn to four additional areas of reality in our personal lives that we need to consider.

It's Not Home

No matter how wonderful the place you are going to serve is, it won't be home—at least not initially. Home is a place that is familiar, where we feel comfortable, accepted, understood, tolerated, loved, and supported. It's where we belong. Instead, in a new place we initially feel like a stranger. We quickly realize that we are weird. Different. Alien. We are the foreigners! The ways we talk, dress, eat, and act are all strange. We may be touched, stared at, and even laughed at. At times we may feel on trial and misunderstood. And because we don't know the language or understand the culture, we frequently feel left out—conversations buzz around us, people laugh or cry, look worried or happy, and we don't feel a part of it. That's part of the reality that may lead us to do some strange things. We develop homesickness and miss things we scarcely even liked "back home" (blizzards, expressways, registration lines at college, TV ads, even cafeteria food).

It's Not a Haven

In addition, going to the mission field is not a haven. It's not a place to run in order to escape—problems, work, school, responsibility, rules and authority, even bad habits, family, friends, or temptations. The reality is that we will discover the same challenges in the mission field that we hoped to leave behind. Temptations abound. Problems are everywhere. We still have to work and carry responsibilities, and we may discover that the rules and authority of another culture are even more difficult to cope with than our own. It's true, "You can run, but you can't hide."

It's Not Heaven

Besides not being home or a haven, the mission field is also not heaven. What does this mean? Well, for starters it means that we won't automatically become deeply spiritual people. Flying over salt water (or driving to another country) won't bring us closer to God. We won't automatically want to get up at 4 a.m. to pray and read our Bibles. We won't automatically get holy just because we are now missionaries.

The reality is that staying close to God in many ways is as difficult overseas as it is at home. But because we are cutting ourselves off from our normal support systems and are putting ourselves "out on a limb" with God, there will certainly be increased opportunities to "taste and see that the Lord is good" if we choose to face our challenges with Him (instead of alone).

It's Not Hell

Lastly, the mission field is not hell. The day comes when that initial excitement has worn off, the bubble bursts, and we wake up one morning and say, "What in the world am I doing here? Why did I think this was a good idea?" Looking longingly at a calendar, time seems to stretch endlessly into the future, and we wonder if we can survive another day, let alone another year! What happened to our sense of well-being and the wonderful joy we anticipated in our dreams of mission service? What kind of reality is this? Is it worth it? The discomfort we feel is a reality we don't enjoy.

So What Do We Do?

Having looked briefly now at the four H's of reality, let's now discuss how to handle them. To begin with, it is important that we expect reality to be different from our dreams and anticipation. Just being forewarned is helpful. At least it helps us avoid the unpleasant surprise of the unexpected. Along with that, we need to begin to actually expect (and enjoy) the unexpected. We frequently discover a new reality that is vastly different and even better than the one we originally expected.

Above all, start a collection of memories. Even on the darkest days when reality seems overwhelming, there are memories to be made and remembered. After all, this truly is an adventure—possibly the greatest adventure you've had to date. Make the most of it. Lastly, keep your eyes on Jesus—the first volunteer missionary in the Christian era. Can you imagine what it was like for Him to cope with the realities of this earth? We really can't even imagine, can we? He made it, and He's promised to be with us always, so we can make it too.

In conclusion, remember that no matter how much discomfort this experience may at times bring you, you will be much closer to true reality during the next weeks and months than you are today. You are going to be reaching out to the real world where you will encounter life in all its reality—diversity, need, pain, joy, hope, and fear—to a degree you've never known it. As a result, your reality will be forever changed. Go in peace!

Your Turn

1. What are some ideas you have about mission and missionaries that are probably unreal stereotypes?

2. Can you think of some things you could do to develop a more realistic view?

Chapter 17

Staying Healthy

Health of body is important to cross-cultural service. The better you feel, the better you can perform what you came to do. Your mental state is often related to how well you are doing physically. Good health contributes to happy attitudes and vice versa.

Some of you are undoubtedly too concerned and worried about your health. You should be assured that overall you are generally at no greater risk during your time of cross-cultural service than you would be doing something similar at home. Some of you may not be concerned enough about your health. You probably need this chapter more than some others! What is crucial is that a balanced view is important to success.

 **Think About It**

Your Concerns

- What are your major health concerns?
- Have you taken time to deal with them?
- What do you need to do before you depart?

Your Special Needs

- Do you have any special needs in relation to your health?
- Do you require a special diet or certain foods?
- What are your allergies?
- Do you require hard-to-find medications?
- Do you require medications that must be stored at prescribed temperatures, for example, insulin?
- Do you need certain supplies, like contact lens solution?
- Have you made plans to care for these things?

Health Facts

Many people are concerned about the wrong things when they think about the health problems missionaries face. While they can occur, major health problems are not usually

- Exotic diseases
- Tropical parasites
- Snake bites
- Large cockroaches

Instead, the number-one killer of missionaries is accidents. Traffic laws and customs differ widely. Driving conditions in many countries are less than ideal. Care in driving and riding is crucial. Motorcycles are especially hazardous and avoidance of night travel is best. Building and construction accidents are also common. Use care and don't take risks.

Weather

Climate—Radical climate changes affect us physically. Many missionaries go to very hot and/or humid climates. Lack of air conditioning and/or heating can have serious effects unless you learn to cope. If you have lost sleep because of the humidity, you cannot expect to accomplish as much as you hoped. Pace yourself.

Sun—Sunburn in a tropical climate can be swift, painful, and debilitating. If you are going to be in the sun, be sure to have sun screen and a hat. Dehydration can also be a problem, and intake of adequate fluids must be planned for.

AIDS

AIDS is a major problem in many countries. Great care needs to be taken in handling the blood and bodily fluids of others. If you are doing medical and/or dental work, or even just first aid, know the rules and wear gloves.

Needles—It is good to supply your own needle if you need an injection. Better yet, don't get any injections if at all possible. Blood transfusions should be received only if you have no other option. Then you should take all the precautions possible, which may include finding your own donor from among those you can trust.

Illicit sex—It should go without saying that for Christians illicit sex is forbidden. Not only is it sin, but in today's world it is foolhardy and a very high-risk behavior.

Inoculations

You will undoubtedly get a list of required immunizations/vaccinations from the organization that is sending you. By all means, follow it! We are fortunate today to have vaccinations/immunizations for many diseases that were previously serious problems—cholera, typhoid, tetanus, polio, rabies, yellow fever, some types of encephalitis, meningococcal meningitis, and hepatitis A and B are the main ones. Not all of these are required for every area, so double-check with your sending organization to be sure you have the ones needed for the specific area to which you are going.

Malaria

Even after we've had the necessary inoculations, we know that there are still some dangerous illnesses we might encounter. One of the most serious is malaria. As you know, malaria is a very real problem in certain tropical areas. The incidence of malaria has been reduced in many areas today—especially cities. However, there are still pockets in many tropical countries where malaria continues to be a serious problem and is therefore something that cannot be treated carelessly. Fortunately, malaria is treatable, especially if diagnosed and treated early. An even better plan is to avoid it. If malaria is a common problem in the area where you will be serving (or traveling for any length of time), there are several important things you can do.

Since malaria is transmitted by a mosquito, one of the most important things you can do is try to avoid being bitten by mosquitoes. The female anopheles mosquito, which carries malaria, generally bites only at night, so you should take extra precautions at night. Wear clothing that covers your legs, arms, and feet, use insect repellent (with DEET, if possible) on your skin and clothes, sleep in a protected place—either a room with good window screens or under a mosquito net that has no holes and has been treated with an insect repellent.

In addition, you may want to take a prophylactic medication to keep you from getting malaria even if you are bitten, especially if you are in an area where malaria is a severe problem. The type of prophylactic prescribed depends on where you are. Check with your doctor or a health professional knowledgeable about the country where you are going for their recommendations. Some people may have unpleasant side effects from malaria prophylactics. In that case, they may prefer to use caution in avoiding mosquito bites and then treat malaria immediately, vigorously, and correctly if they should get it.

Food Safety

Most of us are interested in eating on a relatively regular basis; thus, the prospect that we may be unable to find food that is safe to eat is cause for some real concern. Due to the hot weather in many parts of the world, varying degrees of care in following hygienic practices, and the presence of different strains of "bugs" to which our systems are not accustomed, it is easier to get sick from eating foods in a new place than it is at home. So, what can you do, aside from preparing all your own food (a pretty unrealistic idea)?

Since most bacteria that cause illness are destroyed by heat, one of the best guidelines is to eat food that is well-cooked—preferably eating it "hot off the stove." Since food is often prepared on the spot, this is a real possibility. Foods that are dry (especially if they are prepackaged and sealed) are also much less likely to be contaminated than foods that are moist.

Some Things to Avoid
- Raw foods (salads, pre-peeled fruits, etc.)
- Foods with a high sugar content—they provide a good culture for bacteria to grow in, especially if they are warm and moist
- Food that has been sitting around uncovered, thus inviting flies and other insects to land on it with their contaminated feet
- Milk products that are not from companies that are known to follow hygienic procedures in the processing

It's true that the local people and some of the "old-time" missionaries may eat all kinds of things that you probably should not eat—especially when you first arrive. Your immune system is not ready to deal with a lot of new "bugs" at first. Gradually you will probably develop some immunities that will enable you to be a bit more adventuresome, but "being safe rather than sorry" is good advice for a newcomer.

Drinking Water and Other Fluids

In most areas the major food problem is not contaminated food. It is water and liquids. Rarely is the "natural" water safely drinkable. Untreated water often contains harmful bacteria, viruses, and parasites such as amoeba that can cause serious and/or long-term problems.

Bottled water—A possible solution, depending on where you get the bottles! When using bottled water, check that the bottle is appropriately sealed and that you personally break the seal. In some places, however, even the local bottled water is not safe.

Ice—Unfortunately, the same holds true for local ice. On a hot day it can be hard to resist, but you may regret your indulgence.

Water Safety

It is very important for you to drink a lot of liquid, but at the same time, the water supply in many places is less than safe. What can you do?

- Use some kind of chemical treatment of the water. Various kinds of water purification tablets are on the market, and most work fairly well if they are fresh. Adding five drops of iodine (Lugol's solution) to a liter of water kills most bacteria. Alternatively, you can also use unscented chlorine bleach in the same proportion. Allow solutions to stand 30 minutes before drinking.
- Boil the water. Be sure that it comes to a rolling boil and stays that way for at least 10 minutes.

- Buy bottled water if you can find some that is safe. (Buy only bottles that are sealed, from companies that have a reputation for safety.)
- Drink bottled drinks, especially sodas from international companies that have a worldwide reputation to protect.
- Drink tea. In many countries "tea" (which may be made from real tea leaves or other plants) is a very safe alternative to water. It has been boiled, is usually very weak, and is in covered containers so tends to be safe.

What to Do If You Get Diarrhea

Though it is important for you to take reasonable precautions, the chances are that at some time you'll probably get some kind of a gastrointestinal upset. The most common type is referred to as "traveler's diarrhea," a self-limiting illness that lasts a few days and is most commonly caused by a form of *E.coli* bacteria. Having diarrhea is never pleasant or convenient, but it can actually be a good thing, since it is the body's way of getting rid of "the bad bugs." The most important thing for you to do initially is to avoid getting dehydrated. If you are able to drink liquids, keep drinking (or sipping if you are also nauseated).

Rehydration drink (recipe next page) is good if packets or bottles of commercially-prepared rehydration fluids are not available. If the symptoms continue for more than two days in adults (children may become seriously dehydrated in much less time) or if symptoms of serious dehydration occur, you may need to see a doctor (if one is available) or bring out the "bigger guns"—antibiotics (e.g., Cipro, Bactrim, etc.) and medications that stop the symptoms by stopping the diarrhea (e.g., Pepto Bismol, Imodium, Lomotil). Obviously, any diarrhea that continues longer than a few days, or is accompanied by bloody stools and/or fever, should be treated by a doctor and may even require hospitalization.

Oral Rehydration Drink

1 liter of purified (boiled, if necessary) water
2 Tablespoons of sugar
1/4 teaspoon of salt
1/4 teaspoon of bicarbonate of soda (or another 1/4 tsp of salt if bicarbonate of soda is not available)
1/2 cup of orange juice or a squeeze of lemon (for potassium replacement and taste)

Crime

Violent crime is probably not a great concern in most mission locations. On the other hand, rip-offs, scams, and petty theft abound in many places. Your mental health can be ruined temporarily by such things. Any incident should be reported and the appropriate counseling received.

Women—In many places women who go places alone are considered fair game. There is safety in numbers. Don't be presumptuous and test your guardian angels!

Taxis—Both men and women should be cautious when taking taxis. Whether the motive is robbery or rape, taxi drivers have been known to take advantage of foreigners in many countries. Traveling in groups is an obvious precaution. Avoiding taxi travel at night is another. And for women, *never* getting into a taxi alone is very wise advice.

A Sample First-Aid Kit

Here is what Maranatha Volunteers International suggests its groups take along on a short-term mission project. Ideally, a physician is a member of the group and can attend to medical needs. Some groups may have a nurse with them. Others have people skilled in various levels of medical expertise. Certainly a first-aid kit should be part of the group luggage.

Items to be included in a standard first-aid kit include:

- Antibiotics—although it is expensive and requires a prescription, Cipro is preferred because it covers the major dysentery pathogens (except amoebas), does not cause sun-sensitivity as do some antibiotics, and has few side effects
- Ace bandage strips
- Aloe Vera or anything with Benzocaine (for severe sunburn)
- Aspirin
- Band-aids
- Bandages–telfa pads and tape
- Benadryl for allergies
- Cling tape (optional)
- Cotton balls
- Female hygiene items (e.g., sanitary pads/tampons)
- Gloves (always wear them when handling blood or other bodily fluids)
- Hydrogen peroxide or Betadine (for sterilizing/cleaning)
- Insect repellent with DEET, 30% strength
- Motrin or Advil provided there is no contraindication (for sore muscles that aren't accustomed to working quite this hard or in this way)
- Needles (to clean out dirt, splinters, or sand under the skin)
- Pepto Bismol (for first stages of intestinal blowouts)
- Polysporin (skin ointment for infections)
- Saline solution (for eye wash)
- Sore throat lozenges (from cold morning air, eating dust, too much talking, etc.)
- Steri-strips (optional)
- Sun screen (minimum of SPF 15; SPF 30-45 is preferred)

First-Aid Medications

Cold Medicines

Tussi-Organidin—Non-narcotic cough syrup.

Hucotuss—Narcotic cough syrup, will cause drowsiness.

Ru-Tuss—Antihistamine/Decongestant, non-sedative, 3 times a day.

Ventolin Inhaler—For asthma or allergic breathing problems, two huffs every hour as needed. This should be prescribed by a physician.

Anti-Itch Medicines

Benadryl—Antihistamine, for hives, causes drowsiness, 1-2 every 6 hours.

Lidex Cream—For non-fungal itchy rashes, 2-3 times a day.

Lotrimin Cream—Fungal rashes like athlete's foot, 2 times a day.

Pain Medicines

Anaprox DS—Non-narcotic-analgesic/anti-inflammatory, may cause ulcers, take with food, 2-3 times a day.

Vicodin—Narcotic analgesic, causes drowsiness, 1-2 every 6 hours. Physician prescribed only because it is habit forming.

Water Safety

Water purification tablets

Stomach Problems

Tagamet or other similar medications—Ulcer pain, also non-sedating anti-itch pill, 2 times a day.

Imodium—Anti-diarrheal, 1 tablet after each stool, maximum of 12 per day. Allow nature to clear toxin from body prior to use.

Compazine—Anti-nausea, use only after stomach contents empty and still retching, 1 tablet every 6 hours.

Antibiotics (Note: allergies do occur)

PCE—Erythromycin, good for bronchitis, skin, strep throat, 2 times a day (newer formulations may be given on a once a day basis).

Amoxil—Penicillin derivative, good for elderly with bronchitis, bladder infections, 3 times a day.

Cipro—Broad spectrum antibiotic, good for bacterial diarrhea, skin infections, serious infections like pneumonia and recurrent urinary tract infections. Dosing frequency is usually 2 times a day. NOTE: may cause diarrhea.

Adapted from *Maranatha Guide to Adventure.*

Important Resources

One of the most authoritative sources of information on health concerns in international travel is the Centers for Disease Control and Prevention's book *Health Information for International Travel* (there is an updated edition each year), Atlanta, Georgia: U.S. Department of Health and Human Services, Public Health Service, HHS Publication No. (CDC) 95-8280. Check the CDC website (www.cdc.gov) for updates.

Remember that the best places to find out any special information about immunizations and particular health advice are your mission organization, your physician, travel clinic, or health department. Immunizations may be required for entry into some countries.

In the case of illness or accident or other trauma, do not delay in seeking professional help including from the office of the General Conference Health Ministries. The General Conference nurse can be contacted by phone (301) 680-6702 and fax (301) 680-6707. The nurse will know how to contact the General Conference Health Ministries director.

Chapter 18

Building
Missionary
Relationships

Historically, most student missionaries, volunteers, and sizeable numbers of career missionaries served as single missionaries. Today, the majority of career missionaries and more and more volunteer missionaries are going to the mission field as married couples, often accompanied by children. Some of you reading this book will go to the mission field single. Others will go as families. But, whether or not you take a family with you, you are still a member of a family; and you will, most likely, become part of a network of missionary families on arrival.

 **Think About It**

- What are the benefits and challenges of mission life for single missionaries? For married missionaries?
- How can missionaries maintain good relationships with the families they leave behind and build supportive relationships with the missionary families they work with?

In the next two chapters we will begin to address some issues in missionary relationships and family life. However, missionary relationships cover much more than can be discussed here. If you would like to explore this topic more deeply, look through the resources list at the end of part 4 for helpful books on singleness and family relationships.

Living in a Fishbowl

One of the surprises that awaits many missionaries when they arrive on the field is the fishbowl experience. Because you are a foreigner, probably look different from the local people, arrive with clothing and other possessions not common in the community, and just generally stick out, you may find yourself the object of a lot of curiosity. You may feel like you are living in a fishbowl with every act, word, and mistake observed, remarked upon, and reported abroad. One of the results of living in the fishbowl is scrutiny of all your relationships, especially your family relationships. In many cultures the family is the center of society, so it is inevitable that missionary family relationships would be of interest to the local community. As a consequence, the way missionaries conduct their personal life, relationships with other missionaries, and their family relationships greatly influences the level of acceptance and approval they receive.

Don't Lose Touch

When missionaries head off to the mission field, they usually have to say good-bye to family members: mother, father, siblings, grandparents, aunts, uncles. For many of you this will be the first time you will live at such a distance from your family. Yet living far away does not necessarily have to translate into losing touch. Family support and care are often crucial, especially in those first few weeks or months of adjustment. Before you leave, make sure to set up methods of communication with your family. E-mail, phone apps, long-distance calling cards, messaging, even "snail" mail can ease the sense of distance and loneliness that may feel overwhelming to the new missionary. Keeping in touch also helps the family at home pray specifically and participate vicariously in the mission adventures of their loved one.

Unwanted Baggage

Leaving behind your extended family and friends does not mean you are leaving behind the hurts, grudges, or poor communication patterns of those relationships. Baggage from the past is never lost on the airplane! In order to be ready for positive relationship-building in the mission field, we need to bring healthy closure as we say good-bye to those we love. Reconciliation of past hurts, words of Affirmation, appropriate Farewells, and realistic Thinking about the future can help to build a RAFT that will

---

RAFT

Reconciliation—In order to leave with a clear mind and heart, we need to make sure that we have made right any wrongs, asked forgiveness, offered forgiveness, and done all in our power to heal any broken relationships.

Affirmation—Giving words of encouragement and thanks to those who have made a difference in our lives not only affirms them but also helps to cement the good memories that we want to carry with us.

Farewells—For healthy closure and successful transitions we must not neglect to say proper and intentional good-byes as we leave—to people, of course, but also to places, pets, and possessions.

Think destination—We all have expectations of what life will be like when we move. We need to identify, think about, and talk through our expectations to make sure they are realistic, neither too high nor too low.

Adapted from Pollock, D. C., & Van Reken, R. E. (2001). *Third Culture Kids: The Experience of Growing Up Among Worlds.* Boston: Nicholas Brealey Publishing.

---

cement the relationships we are leaving behind and carry us expectantly toward new ones.

The Single Missionary

Single missionaries have a unique place in the history of mission. Paul, the great missionary writer of much of the New Testament, worked as a single missionary. In fact, being unmarried according to Paul, has some benefits. He argued in 1 Corinthians 7:29-35 that singleness is to be preferred in these last days of earth's history. Unmarried people are more able to concentrate on things of the Lord and are spared some of the cares of this world—two reasons he gives for remaining single. So, if you are going to the mission field as a single person, you are following in the footsteps of many outstanding missionaries from Paul on down through the ages.

Probably you can think of a few more reasons why being a single missionary has its benefits. To begin with, a mobile lifestyle is just easier and less complicated when there is only one person to consider. More time is available for mission, and the cost of airplane tickets for one person, not to mention other expenses, is considerably less than for a family. As Paul says, singles have more freedom to serve the Lord without also having to attend to the needs of a spouse.

Meet the Challenge

Of course, along with those benefits come some unique challenges for single missionaries. Loneliness is, perhaps, one of the biggest. Because of cultural and language barriers, singles may feel that there is no one to talk to who can really understand. In cultures where adults rarely remain single, unmarried missionaries may find that they are easily misunderstood. Why would a healthy, well-educated person remain single? There must be something wrong with them, goes the reasoning. They may be considered without authority or seen as less trustworthy just because they are single. They may have to constantly fend off matchmakers and marriage proposals. They may be faced with seductive behaviors and flattering offers.

Sometimes loneliness and constant temptation can lead to unwise, even dangerous, behavior. Dating practices are very cultural, and single missionaries can easily mishandle romantic advances. The safest policy, and one that most Adventist organizations follow, is no dating while on the mission field. If single missionaries feel a romantic attachment forming, they need to seek the counsel of other missionaries and church leaders. Usually it is best if they return to their home country to gain some perspective on the relationship before making a permanent decision.

Get Adopted

One excellent antidote for loneliness is finding an adopted family to join. In many cultures adding one more "niece" or "nephew" to family gatherings is a natural and expected part of family life. Other missionary families can also provide a home away from home for single missionaries. "I never had to spend a holiday alone," one single missionary who spent 23 years in the mission field stated. "Some family from church or work always invited me to be part of their family celebrations."

While nurturing and enjoying family relationships, single missionaries must be careful to guard their adopted family's privacy and family time. Good boundaries are important. Likewise, families should not take for granted that single missionaries will fulfill all the roles of a relative, such as providing unlimited babysitting services or giving financial support. Probably, the best solution for single missionaries is to develop relationships with several families, among both nationals and missionaries. Having a larger support system makes maintaining appropriate boundaries easier and ongoing fellowship possible.

Getting Too Much Attention?

One of the hazards of living cross-culturally may be the kind of attention you receive. Especially if you are young and single, but sometimes even if you are married, you may arouse considerable interest among those of the opposite sex in your new community. Remember that appropriate relationships between genders are very culturally defined. What may seem normal friendliness to you may be viewed as sexual enticement in another culture. What feels like sexual harassment to you may be tolerated behavior in your host culture.

Unwanted attention may also come from those who are acting in ways generally disapproved by their culture. They get away with their bad behavior because you do not have the usual protection (e.g., brothers or a father who will defend you) or because you seem so exotic that normal social restraints do not apply. While there is little you can do to change the local view of foreigners or completely eliminate such behaviors as inappropriate touching while on crowded buses or sexual offers hollered across the street, there are a few things you can do to help diminish unwanted attention.

- Learn about and model your behavior on the way good Christian adults act in that culture, e.g., appropriate body language, dress, amount of eye contact, language used between genders, etc.
- Avoid compromising situations and unsavory places—generally travel, work, and socialize in groups.
- Seek to understand the full range of gender relationships in the culture before judging, either positively or negatively, an individual behavior. Sometimes when seen in the light of the whole culture, behaviors take on different meanings.
- Discipline your mind to dwell on wholesome thoughts, and make sure your motives and heart are pure in all relationships.

If you are harassed at work or cannot deal with the inappropriate attention you receive in the community, seek advice from your supervisor or other trusted church leader. Do not blame yourself and/or dismiss the incident(s) as imaginary or unimportant. Harassment and abuse do occur and need to be dealt with immediately and forthrightly.

Need help but no one to talk to? Contact the Institute of World Mission (iwm@gc.adventist.org) for confidential support, counseling referrals, or other available help.

Your Turn

1. In this chapter we discussed how to make a good transition to your new life by building a RAFT. Write ideas below of who you need to talk to as you follow each step.

   a. Reconciliation

   b. Affirmation

   c. Farewells

   d. Think destination

2. How do you feel about "living in a fishbowl?" What will be your response to interest in your personal life?

3. Review the benefits and challenges of being a single missionary. Can you think of other benefits or challenges mission service brings to single missionaries? What would you like to see done to help make mission service less lonely for single missionaries?

Chapter 19

The Missionary Family

I can remember how excited I was when, as a teenager, I boarded the plane headed to Africa with my parents. And I remember how exhausted I felt, many years later, when my husband and I made the same trip with two small children. Taking a family to the mission field really is an adventure, but it has an upside and a downside.

Many of you are heading to the mission field with your family. Sharing the adventure of mission with those you love is wonderful. Family members provide ready-made support for each other. There is someone to talk to in the home language and someone to share the new experiences with. As the old proverb says, "Joys shared are doubled, and problems shared are halved." However, missionary families also face a more complicated adjustment task. Packing, traveling, and settling in involve more people and, therefore, require more relational energy. Most missionaries, however, would agree that despite the difficulties, complexity, and, yes, even exhaustion, there is great joy and fulfillment in serving God as a missionary family.

 **Think About It**

- How does the decision to be a missionary affect your family? Your spouse? Your children?
- Does each family member sense God calling them individually to mission?
- What are some of the factors that might make moving to the mission field complicated for your family?

Family Transition

Moving to the mission field is one of the biggest and most complex moves a family can make. Not only is the family physically relocating; they are also transitioning emotionally, culturally, and socially. They must adjust to a new lifestyle, social status, language, food, work, and climate.

One of the results of such a profound transition is a self-centered focus—we are just trying to survive all the changes that are occurring in our lives, and we don't have a lot of energy to spare for others. Having to be involved in a spouse's or a child's adjustment issues can use up more patience and empathy than we feel we have. (Single missionaries who go with a team may feel a similar impatience with a teammate or roommate who is having a difficult adjustment.) Yet families are interconnected systems, so the goal must be an optimal adjustment for each member of the family.

Understanding the transition process, especially its uneven and individual nature, can help missionaries, whether single or married, be more aware of their own adjustment process and sympathetic with the adjustment difficulties of others (see chapter 11 for a discussion of the stages of transition).

The Missionary Marriage

Did you know going to the mission field can benefit your marriage? The knowledge that God has called you as a couple to mission service gives you a shared purpose. In the process of achieving a common goal you will create a shared history and a rich memory bank. Traveling to exotic places, learning to eat and like new foods, making new friendships, even facing hardships together combine to give you a history that is uniquely yours as a couple. Unlike many spouses who have to schedule time together, missionary couples often find that one gift of mission service is more time together. You may work in the same office, eat most of your meals at home, travel everywhere together, and share friends and social activities with your spouse.

A benefit you may only appreciate over time is the freedom you have to create the cultural environment in your family life. In some ways missionaries live outside of both their home culture and their host culture. While they need to fit in with host cultural norms most of the time, in their own home missionaries usually create a hybrid family culture. That hybrid family culture, made up of all the cultures you and your spouse bring to the marriage and experience as a couple, can become a cherished and freeing part of your family heritage.

Facing Challenges Together

As can be expected, mission life also brings challenges to missionary couples. Rather than giving you more time together, you may find that the job you are going to do requires you or your spouse to travel away from home much of the time. Frequent separations, while difficult for marriages everywhere, are particularly challenging to missionary marriages because of the (often) poor communication, dangers of travel, and inadequate support for the spouse left at home.

Other challenges mission service poses for missionary couples may be loss of personal and couple support systems, financial insecurity, and environmental, cultural, or religious differences that impact the marriage: such as lack of privacy, taboos on any public display of affection, differences in gender roles, etc.

You don't have to be married very long before you discover that the challenges of life are frequently mediated through the marriage. Stress at the office or trouble with the children too often shows itself in tension between the spouses. Cross-cultural living brings new kinds of stress, so don't be surprised if it also requires more from your marriage. Yet, just as weight-lifting strengthens muscles, responding appropriately to the challenges of mission living can strengthen missionary marriages.

Of first importance is the fundamental commitment to each other that is foundational to all Christian marriages. If we are committed to the marriage, then we will have the motivation to practice good communication skills, be tolerant and flexible in our responses, pay attention to our spouse's needs, and grow in enjoyment and love for each other. Intentionally working to strengthen your marriage is a gift you give yourself and a powerful witness to the Lord of love.

Strengthening Missionary Marriage
(Ideas gathered from missionaries at Mission Institutes)
- Take walks together to talk over your day.
- Read interesting books out loud to each other.
- Pray with each other daily.
- Play together—table games, soccer, tennis, etc.
- Travel together whenever possible.
- Use Skype to talk for free even when apart.
- Plan a special couple time during annual leave.
- Clear the air of any hurts before bed every night.
- Learn about and show interest in each other's work.
- Read books/watch videos on marriage enrichment.

Third Culture Kids

Many families take children to the mission field, and more are born to missionary families. Estimates vary, but it is not an exaggeration to say that missionary kids (MKs) number in the tens of thousands today. And, missionary kids are part of a larger group of Third Culture Kids (TCKs) that includes military, diplomatic corps, and international business kids. Their "third culture" is a mixture of their parents' culture (first culture) and the various cultures they have grown up in (second culture).

A TCK is defined as "a person who has spent a significant part of his or her developmental years outside the parents' culture. The TCK builds relationships to all of the cultures, while not having full ownership in any. Although elements from each culture are assimilated into the TCK's life experience, the sense of belonging is in relationship to others of similar background" (Pollock & Van Reken, 2001, 19).

Understanding and appreciating the strengths and weaknesses that an international upbringing fosters in TCKs can help parents respond and support their children appropriately. Third Culture Kids are not weird and different. Their problems are human problems, and their gifts are a natural result of their childhood experiences. We, as parents, need to accept that our decision to be missionaries has changed our children's lives forever—not all for the worse and not all for the better. Our task, and theirs as they mature, is to work with God to meet the challenges and build on the benefits their MK experiences provide.

TCK Characteristics

Despite their varied backgrounds, TCKs share many characteristics. A mobile childhood brings sensitivity and empathy for others, a wide relationship bank, and many rich memories. Mobility can also make TCKs feel rootless and experience grief at the loss of belongingness. They are often keen observers with excellent cross-cultural skills, independent, and highly motivated. Their innate flexibility and adaptability can make them appear, however, without convictions, socially slow, and out of step in the parents' culture. In spite of the difficulties, most TCKs are grateful for their international upbringing and the broad worldview it has given them.

What Parents Can Do

One of the greatest gifts missionary parents can give their children is a stable and loving home. Open communication, healthy boundaries, positive community relationships, and a practical faith in God are a few of the parental characteristics that provide a solid foundation for successfully rearing MKs. As missionary parents, we need to understand our children's "TCK-ness" and allow them to experiment as they seek to find their own cultural identity. Creating for our children a familiar home environment, as much as possible, while supporting their development of positive relationships in the host culture, can help them balance their cultures.

Younger children are greatly affected by their parents' adjustment issues. Older children may need help to stay in touch with friends and relatives in the home culture, make new friends, and adjust to a different school environment. By honestly working through our own adjustment issues, by seeking to maintain a strong marriage relationship, and by helping our children feel a valuable part of God's mission, we can trust our Father in heaven to guide us as we parent His kids.

For more about TCKs read the book *Third Culture Kids* listed in Part 4 Resources for Further Study.

Your Turn

1. Which of the suggestions for strengthening missionary marriages seem most helpful to you? What additional ideas can you suggest? Write them below.

2. How has your family dealt with major transitions in the past? What can you do to make this transition process easier for your family?

3. Review the TCK characteristics. Which ones do you feel most concerned about for your children? What can you do to help your children develop the positive characteristics and deal with the negative ones?

Volunteer and Career Missionary Relationships

Building a well-functioning team anywhere takes intentional effort. The diversity of missionary teams, made up of volunteer and career missionaries from many cultural backgrounds and age groups, requires even more patience and persistence to work well. Understanding the differences can be the start to building a missionary team that demonstrates God's love by loving one another.

Volunteer vs. Career

Volunteer missionaries need well-defined jobs that are within their ability to perform. Because of the shorter time frame for their service, they cycle through the stages of transition and culture shock more rapidly. Loneliness may lead them to need more social support or seek questionable relationships. Career missionaries may or may not have their own transition and culture shock issues worked through. Usually they have the competing demands of family and work, making their lives very full and busy. Their adjustment to the local culture over many years may include some conclusions that sound negative or prejudiced or arise from culture fatigue. Volunteer and career missionaries need to recognize that their experiences are very different and resist judging each other.

My Culture vs. Your Culture

As one missionary recently said, "I don't have any trouble with the local people; it's the missionaries from _____ that I can't get along with!" So often the multicultural nature of the missionary team means that missionaries must adapt to several cultures in addition to the local culture. Every missionary team becomes a unique culture of its own made up of the various cultures of its members. Recognize that if there are a number of missionaries from one culture, that cultural style will likely predominate in patterns of communication and conflict management. When new missionaries arrive, their task is to learn not only the local culture but also the team culture. Missionary teams need to constantly remember that their reason for being is to witness to the local people and adjust their team culture to best fulfill that purpose.

Younger vs. Older

Each generation, shaped by different life events, absorbs a unique package of values and beliefs. In addition, the longer one lives, the more one is formed by life's trials and joys. Older missionaries may feel that if they suffered certain trials then younger missionaries should suffer similar trials. Younger missionaries may believe that older missionaries are inflexible and old-fashioned. Older missionaries need to remember what it was like to be young and lonely and far away from home and be willing to provide love and support and acceptance. Younger missionaries need to understand that experience does count for something and that older missionaries can teach them a lot if they are willing to be patient learners.

Part 4 Resources for Further Study

Blomberg, J. R., & Brooks, D. F. (Eds.). (2001). *Fitted Pieces.* St. Claire Shores, MI: SHARE Education Services.

Brewster, T., & Brewster, B. S. (1984). *Language Learning Is Communication, Is Ministry.* Pasadena, CA: Lingua House.

Chapman, G. (2004). *The Five Love Languages: How to Express Heartfelt Commitment to Your Mate.* Chicago, IL: Northfield Publishing.

Davidian, R. D. (1988). *Learn a New Language: A Creative Guide.* Berrien Springs, MI: Center for Intercultural Relations.

Elmer, D. (2006). *Cross-cultural Servanthood: Serving the World in Christlike Humility.* Downers Grove, IL: InterVarsity Press.

Hammond, M. M. (2003). *Sassy, Single, & Satisfied: Secrets to Loving the Life You're Living.* Eugene, OR: Harvest House Publishers.

Kerr, A., & Kerr, D. (2004). *You Know You're an MK When. . .* Order from MK List, 307 Administration Boulevard, Winona Lake, IN 46590.

Knell, M. (2001). *Families on the Move: Growing Up Overseas—and Loving It!* Grand Rapids, MI: Monarch Books.

Laite-Lanham, S. (2010). *Recovering from Traumatic Stress: A Guide for Missionaries.* Pasadena, CA: William Carey Library.

Lingenfelter, J. E., & Lingenfelter, S. G. (2003). *Teaching Cross-culturally: An Incarnational Model for Learning and Teaching* (3rd ed.). Grand Rapids, MI: Baker Academic.

Lingenfelter, S. G., & Mayers, M. K. (2016). *Ministering Cross-culturally: An Incarnational Model for Personal Relationships.* Grand Rapids, MI: Baker Academic.

Livermore, D. A. (2006). *Serving With Eyes Wide Open: Doing Short-Term Missions With Cultural Intelligence.* Grand Rapids, MI: Baker Books.

Pollock, David C., & Van Reken, R. E. (2001). *Third Culture Kids: The Experience of Growing Up Among Worlds.* Boston, MA: Nicholas Brealey Publishing.

Romano, D. (2001). *Intercultural Marriage: Promises & Pitfalls.* Boston, MA: Intercultural Press.

Werner, D., Thuman, C., & Maxwell, J. (1992). *Where There Is No Doctor: A Village Health Care Handbook* (Rev. ed.) Berkeley, CA: The Hesperian Foundation.

Wilson-Howarth, J. (2009). *Essential Guide to Travel Health.* London, UK: Cadogan Guide.

Yehieli, M., & Grey, M. A. (2005). *Health Matters: A Pocket Guide for Working With Diverse Cultures and Underserved Populations.* Yarmouth, ME: Intercultural Press.

Young, A. (2015). *Looming Transitions: Starting and Finishing Well in Cross-cultural Service.* CreateSpace.

5

Sharing Christ in a Different Culture

Chapter 20

Building
Redemptive
Relationships

Because a missionary or a witness is what we are, rather than what we do, it becomes a twenty-four-hour-a-day, seven-day-a-week activity. We are witnessing by the way we dress, by our activities, by our values, and by our priorities. The question of a "target audience," a specific group of people with whom you wish to share Jesus, is almost beside the point. Your "target audience" is everybody around you, particularly those your life touches in normal activity. In this chapter you will begin to identify natural avenues for discipling and natural environments in which to witness.

 **Think About It**

People around you are aware, at least subconsciously, of your values and thus, your loyalties. Stop and reflect on the past 24 hours: What does your clothing, right now, say about your values and self-image? Has your behavior today been seen as patient, kind, and considerate? What parts of your behavior have been seen as impatient, inconsiderate, and unkind? How have your priorities, today, valued others more than yourself?

Discipling

You may need to add a new term to your vocabulary, one that your spell-checker will not recognize: "discipling." Discipling means witnessing to others so they become new Christians or new disciples of Jesus. It involves the entire process from spiritual conception to new birth, and on to becoming a fully mature, self-reproducing Christian. This work does not belong to the pastor; it is your responsibility. Remember, it is not the shepherds who produce new sheep. Sheep make new sheep. Just so, it is not pastors who make new disciples. It is disciples who make new disciples. There are very good reasons for this:

1. You are the one who got to know the person who is becoming a Christian in the first place.
2. You are the one who has introduced the new disciple to Jesus.
3. You are the one the new Christian knows and trusts.
4. You are the most believable example of genuine Christianity the new disciple knows.
5. It is most natural for the new Christian to learn the faith by observing and copying you.
6. This obviously will keep you on your toes as a growing Christian.

Relationship Box Exercise

On the next page you see a group of boxes labeled by the areas of your normal life, boxes in which you generally live and work. This is your personal "network," and, as you will see, evangelism or Christian witness operates best as "network" evangelism.

Within each box write the names of people you meet and talk to at least three to four times a week. These are your primary contacts for Jesus. They are the people who know and trust you, who feel comfortable with you. These are people with whom natural channels of communication have been established. Some degree of relationship has already been established with these people. The issue now is to translate these into redemptive relationships.

Home and Family	Work
Associations	Neighbors & Friends

For many of us, especially longtime Christians, we may find that there are very few names in our boxes that are not already Christians. What can you do to enlarge the number of potentially redemptive relationships? The answer is twofold: be more friendly and make more friends.

How to Relate to Others

As you think about how you can become a more effective soulwinner, consider this statement about the Master Soulwinner.

> Christ's method alone will give true success in reaching the people. The Savior mingled with men as one who desired their good. He showed His sympathy for them, ministered to their needs, and won their confidence. Then he bade them, "Follow me" (White, *Ministry of Healing*, 143).

Here are some practical guidelines for relating to others. Begin practicing these today in all your contacts.

Develop good listening skills—Practice focusing on what people are saying to you, not on what you want to say in return or rebuttal. Listen attentively and ask for clarification.

Establish a personal bond—Face-to-face contact, physical proximity, and eye contact are some of the ways different cultures establish relationships. Relate in ways appropriate to the culture where you are.

Foster an attitude of encouragement—Make people feel good; affirm their good ideas and plans. Don't nag! As the song says, "Accent the positive and eliminate the negative."

Make yourself interesting to others by being interested in them—Be aware of current events, books, films, and music. Develop hobbies that you can share with others. Ask others about themselves. Focus on them, what they do and why, their families, jobs, interests, and what makes life exciting to them. Get them to tell their "story."

Secrets of Effective Witnessing

Earn the right to be a witness by first being a genuine friend. Be natural. Don't attempt to be what you are not. The real you will come through anyway. Don't step in and out of a role.

Don't rush. Remember that there are two ways to get a chicken out of an egg: with a hammer or a little warmth and time. Stimulate interest that leads to questions, then answer them. Be obvious without being offensive. Be a deliberate Christian without making a "big deal" out of it.

Draw attention to the multi-culturalism of Christianity. It is originally an Asian faith with African connections.

Make your point without demanding agreement. People need time and space to reflect on life-changing paradigm shifts.

Jesus saw in every soul one to whom must be given the call to His kingdom. He reached the hearts of the people by going among them as one who desired their good. He sought them in the public streets, in private homes, on the boats, in the synagogue, by the shores of the lake, and at the marriage feast. He met them at their daily vocations and manifested an interest in their secular affairs. (White, *Desire of Ages*, 151)

Ideas for Expanding Your Relationship Boxes

- Take a class (or teach) at a local school or university.
- Join a musical group.
- Join and participate in professional organizations.
- Join and participate in service clubs (e.g., Rotary, Kiwanis, etc.). Many of them are international.
- Attend neighborhood events. Often you do not need an invitation to attend weddings, funerals, baptisms, fiestas, work groups, or sporting events.
- Places to meet people: cafés and coffee houses, tea houses, local markets, fairs and festivals, plazas and parks, bookstores and stalls, flea markets, sporting events, recreation and game areas for soccer games, bird collectors, open-air chess, bocci-ball, etc., etc., etc.
- Note: Be cautious about identifying with political groups or activities.

Remember the can of soup? The more we "open the can of soup," and eat it, the easier it is to share it. Think of the last time you discovered a great new restaurant or a fantastic recipe for pizza. Remember the last time you fell in love. Remember how easy it was to tell others about it?

Your Turn

1. We have talked about being a witness for Jesus. Who is your primary audience right now? How are you witnessing to them? List three steps you can take this week to add non-Christian contacts to your boxes.

2. Can you remember a time when you offended someone to whom you were witnessing? How would you do it better today?

3. Have you ever sensed that you were God's mouth, feet, or hands so that sharing Jesus simply flowed naturally? What happened? Why?

Chapter 21

Preparing Your Testimony

God has not retained many of us as lawyers, but he has summoned all of us as witnesses.

As they flew from Amsterdam to Bombay, an Asian gentleman and a western missionary shared a number of hours of conversation over the usual topics: the airline food, current events and world conditions, family, and work. After a pause the turbaned Asian mentioned that he was returning home for the birthday of Guru Nanak, the last of the great gurus of Sikhism. It was an important date for him and his family, and he returned home from London annually for the event. He went on to describe the basic tenets of the Sikh faith and how it permeated his entire life, from the clothing he wore to the annual celebrations. Then, turning to look the missionary in the eyes, he asked, "Now tell me about Christianity. What do you believe?" The missionary reflected for a moment in prayer and replied....

 **Think About It**

Everyone faces opportunities such as this and must be ready "in season and out of season" to share his or her faith. Where would you begin to answer the Sikh's question? How would his background and faith determine what you would say or how you would couch it? Would your testimony be factual (intellectual, cognitive, doctrinal) or personal (relational, affective)? Why?

How to Become a Missionary

Jesus and His disciples arrived on the other side of Lake Galilee, in the territory of Gerasa. As soon as Jesus got out of the boat, He was met by a man who came out of the burial caves there. This man had an evil spirit in him and lived among the tombs. Nobody could keep him tied with chains anymore; many times his feet and his hands had been tied, but every time he broke the chains and smashed the irons on his feet. He was too strong for anyone to control him. Day and night he wandered among the tombs and through the hills, screaming and cutting himself with stones.

He was some distance away when he saw Jesus; so he ran, fell on his knees before Him, and screamed in a loud voice, "Jesus, Son of the Most High God! What do you want with me? For God's sake, I beg you, don't punish me." (He said this because Jesus was saying, "Evil spirit, come out of this man!")

So Jesus asked him, "What is your name?"

The man answered, "My name is 'Mob' there are so many of us!" And he kept begging Jesus not to send the evil spirits out of that region.

There was a large herd of pigs nearby, feeding on a hillside. So the spirits begged Jesus, "Send us to the pigs, and let us go into them." He let them go, and the evil spirits went out of the man and entered the pigs. The whole herd–about two thousand pigs in all–rushed down the side of the cliff into the lake and drowned.

The men who had been taking care of the pigs ran away and spread the news in the town and among the farms. People went out to see what had happened, and when they came to Jesus, they saw the man who used to have the mob of demons in him. He was sitting there, clothed and in his right mind; and they were all afraid. Those who had seen it told the people what had happened to the man with the demons, and about the pigs. So they asked Jesus to leave their territory.

As Jesus was getting into the boat, the man who had had the demons begged him, "Let me go with you!"

But Jesus would not let him. Instead, He told him, "Go back home to your family and tell them how much the Lord has done for you and how kind he has been to you."

So the man left and went all through the Ten Towns, telling what Jesus had done for him. And all who heard it were amazed (Mark 5:1-20 *Good News Translation*).

Think about this former demoniac who is now a "missionary" to his own people. What sort of tools or budget did this new "missionary" have? How much training did this new "missionary" have? What do you think he said to his family and friends? What were the two components of Jesus' instructions to him? How would these two components look in your story?

Your Own Story

Your story is as real, important, and unique as the story of the healed demoniac. He could not tell the story of others, since he probably didn't know any. He probably was not even Jewish and had no part in the history of God's covenant people. Each person's story is unique, personal, and an account of grace in action.

Remember that witnesses are allowed to tell only what they have seen and experienced. They are not teachers or specialists who are expected to be theological authorities. Remember also that secondhand information is never as reliable as firsthand. In court, secondhand information is never accepted.

You may be a convert with an amazing story of being rescued from a terrible life of sin. Or you may be a "born and bred Christian" who has never known a life apart from Jesus and has never even been tempted to wander from your allegiance to Jesus. Both of these stories are important, grace-filled, and part of the larger picture of what God is doing in this world.

Preparing Your Own Testimony

How do you prepare your own testimony? To get started, return to your life map in chapter eight and reflect for a bit on who you are, where you have come from, and what you have been through. You may wish to redraw the spiritual "map" of your life with "geographical" events such as mountains for high experiences, deserts of despair, flooded rivers of trials, and gardens of delight. Bridges may represent people who have helped you over impasses. Remember, your experience and your life with Jesus are the basis for your testimony.

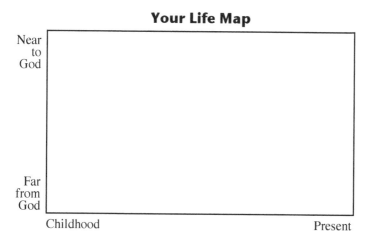

Your Life Map

Here are some common components to a personal testimony:

- Where my story begins.
- What my life was like without Jesus.
- How and where I met Jesus. Who introduced me to Jesus? Any unusual features about the event?
- What changed when I met Jesus and invited Him into my life as Lord and Savior?
- How is my life different now than before I met Christ?
- What Jesus means to me personally and what I value most about the relationship? (Be as specific as possible here.)
- Specific biblical promises or passages that are very meaningful to me.

All of this should take no more than three to four minutes to tell. The objective of sharing this story is to make others "jealous" of your special relationship with Jesus and to create a desire on their part to have a similar relationship.

Contextualizing Your Story

Every storyteller knows that each audience is different and that the story must be "tailored" to fit the audience. Language and style will change with each audience. We call this "contextualization," because each new "context" of telling the story calls for this reshaping of your story.

This suggests that you should seriously reflect on what you know about the faith and culture of the people to whom you are going—their history, main figures and personalities, historic relations with Christianity and with your nation or ethnic group, and the possible bridges between the host faith and Christianity. All of this will be important in contextualizing or reshaping your story.

Be careful, however. Bernard Joinet tells of a well-meaning missionary who, in his attempt to identify with the people to whom he had been sent, called all the people of the village together. He professed his love for them and his determination to be one of them. To dramatize his words and decision to break with his own people, the missionary took out his passport and burned it in front of the shocked onlookers. What was meant as an act of solidarity, however, was not seen that way at all by the villagers. For them he had repudiated his own family and people. He did not, in their minds, know the meaning of love. "He rejects and despises those who gave him life," they said, "who fed and reared him. We can't trust him. He has rejected his father and mother. Perhaps one day he will also reject us whom he calls his brothers!"

Based on "I am a Stranger in My Father's House," *African Ecclesiastical Review 14* (1972): 244-245.

Your Turn

1. Write out the major details of your story. This will help you to choose your words carefully and make it engaging.

2. Now practice telling this story or "testimony." Share it with a Christian friend and ask for his or her reaction and help in perfecting it. Then share it with a non-Christian friend or family member and ask for his or her response.

3. From what you know of your host culture, rewrite your story to make it appealing in that culture.

Chapter 22

Leading Someone to Christ

In this chapter you will learn specific ways to introduce people to Jesus as a personal Savior. As you think about introducing people to Jesus, where do you start? The starting point is trust. It is often very impolite to walk right in with your Bible and your Savior. This is similar to intruding into an ongoing conversation without any sense of what is being discussed. The people do not know you and have no reason to trust you. Your testimony has no value until you have established your commitment to the people in a deep and accepting friendship. Before you can share Jesus, you must earn the right to share Jesus. So ask yourself, "Why should they believe me?"

Before You Begin

Stop and think first about the people to whom you are introducing Jesus. There are frequently significant differences between these people and the people you are used to in your own culture. These differences may include

- *Background*—family, ethnicity, nationality, education, personal history, age

- *Shared history*—the degree to which you both have known each other and shared some of life together, schooling, job, family
- *Core values*—stuff that is really important in this person's life, family, reputation, sports, finances
- *Decision-making style*—individual or group decision-making orientation
- *The manner in which they learn*—visual, audio, cognitive, kinesthetic, affective

Observing these factors should help you to find appropriate ways of introducing Jesus. In addition, you should be aware of other significant cultural differences when you think about leading someone to Jesus.

Other Differences

1. *Motives to seek salvation.* Much of Western society is a guilt-based society. Westerners sense personal guilt for sins and shortcomings. Other societies are shame-based. They do not have a sense of personal guilt, but rather one of collective shame. Thus they may sense their shame within their family or clan or tribe. It is not so much a personal matter, but a collective matter. Generally shame-based societies are more prone to making collective decisions and, parallel to their lack of a sense of personal guilt, they are very reticent about stepping out individually. In fact, such an individual act would produce a strong sense of shame at moving contrary to, or opposed to, their collective way of life (or manners). Here the strongest decisions for Christ are made in the group.

2. *Where do you start?* In the Western model people are generally introduced to the Scriptures first and then to God the Father, the Son, and the Holy Spirit. After that they study various doctrines and practices of the Bible as understood by the Seventh-day Adventists, as well as many other Christians. In many other cultures the first question is, "How can I experience the power of God?" They want to know your own personal

experience with God. Often prayer is a high-priority subject as they begin to experience the God of the Scriptures.

3. *What do you build on?* As you look for a place to connect, it may be well to ask about their sense of need. Where may their faith have failed? Are there redemptive analogies that will enable them to understand biblical concepts? Are there stories and myths, such as the "altar to the unknown god" which Paul used when speaking to the Athenians (Acts 17:22-28)?

4. *Where there is no god.* The western model has presupposed at least some Christian orientation, and colonialism made that orientation seemingly widespread in much of the world. People accepted Jesus because they accepted the Bible. But as many areas of the world become multicultural and secularized or experience growing nationalism, that orientation is no longer so widespread. It can no longer be assumed that people have accepted the Bible as the Word of God. Other living faiths are experiencing similar confusion as western secularism is spread through the media, particularly television. While classic Buddhism can be atheistic or godless, and is mostly a philosophy, secularism is qualitatively different. Secularism is not the denial of God; it is the irrelevance of God. As in formerly Christian lands, in Buddhist, Hindu, and even Islamic countries, there are growing segments of society where the faith is only a thin cultural veneer covering an essentially secular outlook on life.

5. *Order of topics.* In non-Christian cultures different presuppositions must prevail. People generally do not even have a pre-Christian orientation. Be sensitive to a priority of topics. In some situations you might follow a sequence such as Scripture, God, Christ, Holy Spirit, etc. In other situations the sequence might be Christ, God, Holy Spirit, Scriptures, etc.

6. *Introduce them to Jesus first.* Cognitively-oriented western Adventists are more prone to come to Jesus through belief in the Scriptures, while non-western cultures are more prone to be relational and intuitive. It may be best to introduce people first to Jesus and after that to

the Scriptures. They will accept Jesus on the basis of your testimony, and they will accept the Scriptures on the basis of their commitment to Jesus.

7. *How do people become Christians?* There are at least four major paths to faith in Jesus:

The faith of the group or family. This is particularly true for many Christians who were born into Christian families. In some group-oriented societies, it is common for whole families to convert (Acts 16:33; 1 Corinthians 1:16) and the conversion is generally more lasting than the conversion of one against the wishes of the family. By pressing for individual conversion you may win one but lose (alienate) many.

A relationship with a Christian. The saying is common but true, "Christianity is caught, not taught." If one does not have confidence in the messenger, the message may not be accepted either. The greater the distance between the messenger and the listener, the less likely a personal relationship of credibility and trust will develop.

Dreams and visions. While God is more than eager to use us in the process of winning others to faith in Jesus, He is not limited to our cooperation. As God spoke to Cornelius directly through dreams and visions (Acts 10:1-8), He still speaks to people today. But He then often brings them in contact with His own people for further help.

Crisis event. Wars, famines, floods, and other natural disasters, as well as personal crises, frequently result in a "failure of faith" and an openness to a new object of faith and devotion. People in the former Soviet Union, especially in central Asia, as well as in China and elsewhere, experienced a vacuum of faith and meaning that had to be filled. If Christians cannot fill that void, too often it is filled by cheap substitutes (e.g, materialism, nationalism, addictions, etc.).

Most people in this world do not share our Christian history or presuppositions. Issues such as differing theories of inspiration and different canonical lists, and even denominationalism, are foreign and irrelevant to them. Faith is more concrete and less abstract. The important question is, what can Jesus do for my life and my group, right now?

Often they will accept Jesus on the basis of the testimony of your personal experience, and the clear indicators in your life of the reality of that experience. Your humble life, your spiritual commitment, and faithful walk with Christ are a convincing foundation that will allow the Holy Spirit to empower anything you verbally say to them.

After Your Testimony

Once you have shared your testimony, it may be appropriate to ask your listener for his/her response. Remember there are direct and indirect societies. Moreover, in most non-western societies, an act of commitment will require the decision of a larger group. You may wish to frame your questions accordingly:

- Does my experience of a personal God make sense in the context of your faith?
- Is an experience such as mine possible in the context of your faith?
- I don't think that my God is a local or western God. How has He been active in your faith history?

If your friend seems particularly open to what you are saying, you may wish to become more direct. Do not be afraid of a direct question. Your friend may be waiting for it. You may wish to ask your friend:

- "Jesus met these needs (be specific) in my life. Do you think He could do the same for you?"
- "Jesus has become my personal friend as well as Savior. Would you like to get acquainted with Him also?"
- "Jesus has brought tremendous peace to my mind and life and enables me to cope with life's pressures. Would you like to experience that peace and help also?"

Then What?

If your friend says "yes," be prepared to share some short specific "snapshot" stories about Jesus (e.g., the woman at the well, the woman caught in adultery, Jesus with the children, the rich young ruler, the wedding feast, etc.).

If the setting is appropriate, invite your friend to pray with you. The prayer should include something similar to:

- "Jesus, I have just heard about you, and this is new to me...."
- "Jesus, I am willing to give you a chance in my life...."
- "Jesus, I want to get to know you better...."
- "Jesus, I invite you into my life, and I ask you to help me with...."

Some people are nervous about praying, and they may be afraid that they will say the wrong thing and offend God. You may wish to lead them through a prayer, inviting them to repeat it after you. Here is a sample prayer.

> *Lord Jesus, I have just heard about you, and I want to know you. I want you to take away my faults and failures and accept me as your own child. Please come into my heart and mind, as you have promised, and lead my life in this difficult world. Amen.*

Some Helpful Scriptures

Here are some passages of Scriptures that might be helpful to share with your friend(s). Remember that these are offered not on the basis that Scripture is more important than Jesus, but that these are Jesus' own words to His followers.

- Revelation 3:20 "Behold I stand at the door and knock."
- John 1:12 "To those who accept me, I give power."
- John 6:37 "Everyone whom the Father gives me will come to me; I will certainly not reject anyone who comes to me."

If Your Friend Hesitates

If your friend hesitates, he or she does not necessarily reject you or Jesus. It may mean that your friend needs more time to think about it, time to talk with others about it, time to be polite in his or her response, or any number of things.

It is important for you to give your friend the opportunity to think about what you have said. It may be very new. It may be totally outside his or her realm of plausibility. If this person is your friend, then you will continue to be a friend and allow time and space for your friend to reflect and begin what may be a lengthy decision-making process.

Your Turn

Ask your pastor for the opportunity to join him in an evangelistic Bible study, and, if appropriate, to teach one yourself.

Urban Friendships: A Guide for the Beginner

More and more missionaries are called to live and work in cities where over 50 percent of the world's population now live. Here are ten suggestions to help you in building relationships in the city.

- Subscribe to a good local newspaper, and keep abreast of what is happening in your city.
- Find a good local radio station. Check the billboards and subway ads for what is important and new. Information is very important.
- Join a health club or spa. It is a great place to meet people.
- Get to know your neighborhood. Shop locally, take walks, talk with people. Ask them where they come from, how the neighborhood has changed, where to get good help and repairs.
- Join Lyons or Rotary clubs. They are always recruiting new members, and they provide instant friendships and connections. They are worth the expense.
- Be aware of what is current in the media: TV, movies, books, etc. You want to sound intelligent.
- Urban friendships are generally shallow and transient. It takes time for people to learn to trust you.
- Learn the history of your city. Why is it there? Who settled where and when? What is the political history? The economic history? Who has been in charge?
- Urban people generally love their city. Don't talk against it. Enjoy it!
- Learn to cheer for the home teams!

Chapter 23

Helping Christians Grow

If you don't care where you are going, it doesn't matter which direction you take. If you don't care about the finished product, it doesn't matter how you build the design. Because we do care, it is helpful to attempt to envision the final project as you begin to lead the new believer toward a mature faith. In this chapter the student will explore the more difficult and important work of helping new Christians integrate their life and faith.

Think About It

- What do mature believers look like? What do they believe? How do they live?
- Why do you have this picture? Where did you get this picture?

Discipleship

How does one identify a Christian, a disciple of Jesus? Jesus spoke of four essential marks of His followers:

1. A disciple identifies with the person of Jesus, denying self, taking up the cross, and following Jesus (Luke 9:23).

2. A disciple is obedient to the word of Jesus, faithfully holding to Jesus' teaching and living it (John 8:31, 32).

3. A disciple expresses and demonstrates love for all other disciples (John 13:35).

4. A disciple is fruitful in the work of Jesus, producing more disciples (John 15:8-16).

As you work with new Christians, you must model these essential marks and enable your friend(s) to model them also. But we need to explore some indicators of these four marks as they become more fully developed.

Eight Major Indicators of a Mature Faith

The Valuegenesis study, analyzing the maturity level of young people in the Seventh-day Adventist Church, is a useful tool for our purposes. It identified eight major indicators of a mature faith. While these are expressed in very North American terms, they can be translated into a variety of cultural contexts. Maturing in faith means—

1. Trusting in God's saving grace and believing firmly in the humanity and divinity of Jesus.

2. Experiencing a sense of personal well-being, security, and peace.

3. Integrating faith and life, seeing work, family, social relationships, and political choices as part of one's religious life.

4. Seeking spiritual growth through study, reflection, prayer, and discussion with others.

5. Seeking to be part of a community of believers in which people give witness to their faith which supports and nourishes one another.

6. Holding life-affirming values, including commitment to racial and gender equality.

7. Advocating social and global change to bring about greater social justice.

8. Serving humanity consistently and passionately through acts of love and justice.

Some of these indicators are more obvious than others; some are more easily achieved than others. These indicators are not provided as a basis for immediate judgment, but as goals toward which mentors encourage their disciples to move.

How to Encourage Growth in New Christians

As you disciple new Christians and seek to move them toward a mature, self-reproducing faith, you may wish to help them focus on the following:

The lordship of Christ—Jesus Christ must truly be the Lord of the believers' lives. Growing in faith, they must be captivated by the person of Jesus and surrender major areas of life to Jesus' control: their careers, marriage plans, families, possessions.

Bible study—Young believers need to learn to daily read and enjoy the Bible, to study it personally and with others in a group, and to memorize meaningful passages. With individual help, young believers soon learn to feed themselves. The process may take a few years.

Prayer and devotion to God—They need to learn to pray and have a meaningful quiet time of worship daily. They should also be taught to pray for others (a simple prayer list may help), and how to confess sins and to live a life of thanksgiving.

Fellowship and the church—Believers grow in the context of fellowship with other believers. New believers need to belong. They need to learn that the church is their spiritual family (cf. the "one another" passages of the New Testament).

Christian character— Paul labored hard to "present everyone mature in Christ" (Colossians 1:28). Paul's goal of Christlikeness is the most essential aspect of discipleship training. This is a lifelong process that builds on the abiding essentials of faith, hope, and love.

Relationships—Discipleship affects all interpersonal relationships (e.g., between family members, employers and employees, the church leaders and members). New believers need to be taught how to apply gospel principles to their relationship with people in the context of their own culture.

Witnessing—Missionaries should teach young believers to share their faith with members of their own family and with friends. This is the most fertile soil for ongoing, fruitful evangelism and church planting.

Social justice—Growing Christians need to learn that the Christian life is personal but never privatized. Christians must, therefore, be concerned about sinful social structures and minister also to the hungry, the homeless, the oppressed, and marginalized.

Adapted and expanded from Jonathan Lewis, ed., 1996, *Working Your Way to the Nations: A Guide to Effective Tentmaking.* Downers Grove, IL: InterVarsity Press.

A Journey Together

Obviously this type of mature faith will take time to develop. As you look at these eight indicators, you may sense a need for growth yourself. As you "disciple" a new Christian, you should begin by confessing that you are still growing also. You may be only a step ahead of the new disciple. But you know where you both are going and how to get there.

Let's think about how to model and teach new Christians in four essential practices of a growing Christian life.

Prayer

Since you are the first model of Christianity for the new Christian, your prayer life becomes a model for his or her prayer life. By instruction and by praying together you introduce the person to different forms of prayer.

Conversation with God—Prayer is the opening of the heart to God as to a friend. Nothing is hidden from God. Everything can be discussed. Nothing will surprise God, drive Him away, or make Him angry.

Worship—In a worship setting prayer is often less personal and more a matter of bringing the community collectively to the throne of God.

Meditation—Prayer is not simply bringing a "shopping list" to God, it is praise and thanksgiving as well as sitting quietly and listening to the voice of God, "when every other voice is hushed" (White, *Ministry of Healing*, 58).

Many forms—Prayer can take on many forms: letter-writing, singing, and playing instruments. Cultures differ in the ways people approach God meaningfully.

Bible Study

The Scriptures are the record of an ancient and ongoing "dialogue" between God and His people about what it means to be the people of God in a variety of times and conditions. As members of the family, we are invited to listen in on this dialogue and to participate.

Casebook vs. cookbook—This "dialogue" suggests that the Bible is not a cookbook with specific "recipes" to produce the same results in any given socio-historical context. The Bible is more a casebook filled with case studies of how God and His people have related to each other. Principles can be drawn from these case studies for the present (1 Corinthians 10:6, 11).

Reading—Regular time spent in reading reliable, clear translations of the Bible acquaints us with this ongoing dialogue, and provokes us to analyze the case studies and apply the principles in our own lives.

Doing—Understanding the Bible is only the first part of Bible study. In Matthew 7:21-27, Jesus reminds us that intellectual knowledge without obedience is totally insufficient.

Fellowship

While there have been cases of isolated Christians surviving without the benefit of fellowship, it is clearly the exception and not the rule. The Scriptures and the whole history of God's covenant people know nothing of a privatized faith, lived apart from and with no regard for the rest of the "family." This fellowship is both a giving and receiving activity and can take at least two different and complementary forms

Small groups—Fellowship really indicates relationship, and this suggests a small group in which the participants encourage each other, support each other, and are accountable to each other. Ideally this group should number between four and twelve persons.

Worship and celebration—Worship and celebration are also aspects of fellowship, and they are often made more intense and satisfying in the context of a larger group or congregation, in which large numbers of Christians blend their gifts and talents in praise to the Father.

Service

Nobody is simply saved. We are all saved from something and for something. Each person born into the kingdom of God is given one or more gifts (1 Corinthians 12:7) and these gifts are given for a purpose, for mission and service. It is imperative that each Christian discover and activate his or her gifts.

Area of service—The arena for the operation of these gifts may be inside the church or outside, but never apart from the church. That is, they may be gifts that are appropriate for worship and service to other Christians (e.g., prophecy or pastoring), or they may be gifts that are needed for the extension of the kingdom of God (e.g., apostleship or missions).

Your role as encourager—As young Christians begin to become involved in prayer, Bible study, fellowship, and service, their gifts will become apparent. It is your responsibility to affirm their gifts and encourage them to seek God's guidance in using them in the mission He has given them.

Your Turn

1. Think about your own Christian journey, and ask yourself who discipled you and encouraged you to grow as a Christian. How was it done? What was most helpful? What do you wish someone had done for you or with you to assist you on your way to Christian maturity?

2. Find a mature Christian from a culture very different from yours. Ask this person to define "spiritual maturity" and tell you how it is achieved. Write out this response and compare/contrast it with your own.

3. If your faith maturity is deemed appropriate, ask your pastor for the opportunity to disciple a new member under his or her guidance.

Chapter 24

"Staying Fit" as a Witness for Christ

A good artisan or mechanic uses the best available tools to produce good results. He actually budgets for new tools, knowing that some will wear out, and newer and improved tools might be available in the future. This is no less true for a missionary. You may have to travel lightly, but don't forget your tools. This chapter introduces you to some of them.

Methods of Studying the Bible

Let's think first about different ways we can read and study the Bible.

Doctrinal Bible Study

This is a topically oriented method of studying the Bible. It focuses on specific teachings and seeks to understand them in the context of the ongoing dialogue that is found in the Scriptures.

A few cautions: the selection of topics is determined by the teacher or the student, not by the Bible. Their theological, denominational, educational, economic, political, and cultural background may determine what is studied and what is left out. To be balanced, this method is best done in community, not alone. Also, be aware of the "proof-text" method of Bible study that takes specific verses or portions out of context. A Bible text must not be made to say something that its context does not support.

Socio-Historical Bible Study

This method of studying the Bible seeks to understand the original socio-historical context of a book or passage and what the text meant to the original listeners. As we listen to the ongoing dialogue in the Bible, we learn essential principles for today.

Eschatological Bible Study

This method looks at Scripture through the lens of the cosmic controversy between Christ and Satan in the light of the final judgment and last-day events. This method is more appropriate for some parts of the Bible (Ezekiel, Daniel, Revelation) than others.

Devotional Bible Study

This common method asks, What is God saying to me now? It seeks personal insights from the various case studies and then applies that message. At its best, this method builds on the other methods.

Relational Bible Study

This method is specifically concerned with application. It is best used in a small group setting where people can hold each other accountable. It specifically asks, How do I (we) apply what I (we) have learned today?

Reading in the Congregation

The Bible was originally written to be read aloud. The text in Revelation 1:3: "Blessed is the one who reads the words of this prophecy, and blessed are those who hear it and take to heart what is written in it," refs to a public reading in the congregation. In Revelation 22:17, 18 a blessing is pronounced on those who "hear" the words of the book. Ask yourself how people might study the Bible without printed copies? How might people study the Bible in a pre-literate society? How might people study the Bible in societies where translations have not yet been made?

Plays and Drama

During the Middle Ages, in pre-literate Europe, morality plays and charades were often used to teach the Scriptures. How might this be adapted today? Imagine what might happen if a group of people were to act out parables of Jesus or healing actions on his part or the story of Zacchaeus the tax collector?

Connecting With the Bible Story

Tom McAlpine (1995) suggests that you should answer three questions as you search the Scriptures:

- What similarities exist between their experience in biblical times and our experience now? (This question leads to contextualization.)
- What light does their experience cast upon our experience? (This leads to prayerful reflection.)
- What should we do about these insights, both as a group and personally? (This leads to actualization.)

The last question forms a bridge to new plans for personal and group action, which helps ensure that the principles of Scripture are lived out obediently and practically.

When you come together for Bible study, make sure that there is accountability for following through on the principles learned. One author recommends the following steps of studying the Bible, implementing the insights gained and sharing the resulting experiences of seeing God at work in one's life:

- *Invite*—As you open the Word of God, remind yourselves that the risen Lord is with you.
- *Read*   – wow, really?
- *View with wonder*—Pick out words or short phrases, read them aloud prayerfully, and repeat them three times.
- *Listen*—Keep silent for several minutes and allow God to speak.
- *Share*—Respond to the question, "Which word has touched me personally?" Do not discuss any contribution, even though some may not share personally but comment instead.
- *Plan for action*—Now discuss any task which the group is called to do in their neighborhood or parish.
- *Pray*
- *Share*—In addition, share with the group next time what God has done in response to obediently putting the truth learned into action. This step should lead to praise and celebration.

Why Are There Different Translations?

There are a number of excellent books available on the merits and problems of various translations and paraphrases of the Bible. We will give here a short summary and evaluation of the main kinds of translations available. Bible translations can be classified in several different ways:

- *Committee translations* avoid personal biases. Translations done by individuals often have more flair and passion than a committee will tolerate. For example, compare Goodspeed's *New Testament* with the *Revised Standard Version*.
- *Literal translations* seek to translate word by word. They appear to be more conservative, more amenable to a concordance.
- *Dynamic translations* seek to understand the larger meaning of a passage and translate that meaning into a dynamic equivalent in the contemporary language of a people.

- *Paraphrases* take the thoughts of the Bible and express them in modern idiom without trying to be a translation. These types of Bibles are usually easy to read, but they are free in their interpretation and thus susceptible to the bias of the paraphraser.

No one approach is better than the other. Used together, they shed light on each other and provide greater insight to the serious student. A basic principle that is consistent with historical Christianity is that people should read the Bible in a translation that uses the latest and best in biblical scholarship and is closest to their own mother tongue.

The New Testament was originally written in Koine Greek. This particular form of Greek was the result of the gathering of an army by Alexander the Great from all the provinces of the Hellenist world, with all their dialects. As these dialects merged into a common (koine) language, this language was spread by this army from Europe to the Indus Valley. It became the common language of all the Greek-speaking world. Far from being a classical language or a "spiritual" language, it was the street language of that age. Ask yourself what translations approximate this form best in your host language?

Bible Study Helps

There are a number of different Bibles and study aids on the market today that make Bible study easier and more reliable. Here are a few of them.

Concordances. There are a number of good concordances on the market, for the KJV, RSV, and NIV Bibles. Strong's Concordance provides the original word in Hebrew or Greek and prevents the student from thinking that one Hebrew or Greek word lies behind a single English word.

Computerized Bibles and helps. If you are using a computer, there are a number of computerized Bibles with concordances, background notes, and other helps that give you great freedom of study and analysis.

Bible lessons. There are a variety of printed Bible lessons and video-taped series. While these may be very helpful in the culture where they were created, they have limited use in other cultures. Great care should be taken when using lessons outside of their culture of origin. It is far better to use Bible lessons created by persons within the host culture or by persons close to that culture.

The Jesus Film. Based on the gospel of Luke, it is a faithful adaptation of the gospel. It has been dubbed into hundreds of languages and used to present the gospel to millions around the world in their own language.

Part 5 Resources for Further Study

Coleman, R. (2006). *The Master Plan of Evangelism.* Grand Rapids, MI: Revell.

Hull, B. (2006). *The Complete Book of Discipleship.* Colorado Springs: NavPress.

Mallouhi, C. (2004). *Mini-skirts, Mothers & Muslims: A Christian Woman in a Muslim Land.* Grand Rapids, MI: Monarch Books.

Mayers, M. K. (1987). *Christianity Confronts Culture: A Strategy for Crosscultural Evangelism.* Grand Rapids, MI: Zondervan.

McAlpine, T. H. (1995). *By Word, Work, and Wonder: Cases in Holistic Mission.* Monrovia, CA: MARC.

Moreland, J. P., & Muehlhoff, T. (2007). *The God Conversation: Using Stories and Illustrations to Explain Your Faith.* Downers Grove, IL: InterVarsity Press.

Newbigin, L. (1986). *Foolishness to the Greeks.* Grand Rapids, MI: Eerdmans.

Pippert, R. M. (1999). *Out of the Saltshaker.* Downers Grove, IL: InterVarsity Press.

Sahlin, M. (1990). *Sharing Our Faith With Our Friends Without Losing Either.* Hagerstown, MD: Review and Herald.

Samaan, P. G. (1990). *Christ's Way of Reaching People.* Hagerstown, MD: Review and Herald.

Simpson, M. L. (2003). *Permission Evangelism: When to Talk, When to Walk.* Colorado Springs, CO: NexGen.

Steffen, T. (2007). *Reconnecting God's Story to Ministry: Cross-Cultural Story Telling at Home and Abroad.* Downers Grove, IL: InterVarsity.

White, Ellen G. (1942). *The Ministry of Healing.* Mountain View, CA: Pacific Press. One of the most powerful presentations of Christ's mission and ministry.

The Jesus Film. Possibly the most translated film in the history of humanity, this film, based on the gospel of Luke, is a powerful cross-cultural resource to present the gospel to millions around the world in their own language. Contact the Jesus Film Project at 1-800-432-1997 for further information, or look online at www.JesusFilmStore.com.

6

How to Be Prepared

Chapter 25

How to Do an Area Study

You are about to embark on a journey to a new land where you will be surrounded by a new culture. When you arrive, you should expect to sometimes be confused by what is going on around you. Cultures differ in degrees of "strangeness" to you. But there are a number of steps you can take that will prepare you for this journey.

Take a trip to your closest library. If you live near a college or university, take advantage of their library. If your community library is small, check out the local high-school library. At the library, do not waste time wandering about. Go directly to the Reference Librarian and explain what you need. Generally there are many resources that can be consulted, with the most current information often found on the internet.

Gathering Your Information

The following pages list some of the questions and items you will want to explore. As you gather the appropriate data, you may want to use a few categories to sort the information. You can download an area study form to fill out at the Institute of World Mission website (www.instituteofworldmission.org).

The Land

- I am going to the country of
- On the continent of
- The climate is
- Some natural resources are
- Its major trade is in: imports/exports/currency

Health and Living Conditions

- Major health risks in the country are
- Availability of hospitals and medical services
- Some local dietary practices
- Eating and drinking precautions
- The national holidays
- Security Issues

The Population

- Size of population
- Demographics

  ____ % of the population is under 18 years old

  ____ % of the population are women

  ____ % of the population is urban (lives in cities)

- The national languages are
- The language of the people group I will be working with is
- Obvious people groups are
- Hidden people groups (e.g., immigrants) are
- General education level

    For men

    For women

- Education is available to
- Barriers to education

Transportation

- Common methods of transportation within the country
- Weekly flights in and out of the country

How Is Society Organized?

- Social groups
- Castes
- Tribes
- Clubs
- Relations between sexes
- Leadership determined and recognized by

Common Customs I Should Know Upon Arrival

- Forms of greetings
- Forms of farewell
- How to say "no" and "yes"
- Serious "no-no's" or taboos

Useful Expressions

- Hello!
- Good bye!
- Please and thank you
- How are you?
- My name is
- How do you say ...?
- Where is the toilet?
- How do I get to ...?

Food

- What is commonly eaten? And when?

- How do people eat?
- What specific areas will I have difficulty with? Why?
- Is eating merely a utilitarian affair or a highly social matter?

History

- Where do the people come from and why?
- Their myths of origin
- Their traditional friends and enemies
- Was this country ever a colony? Of which nation?
- Date and circumstances of independence
- Membership in international, political, or trade organizations
- Involvement in recent conflicts and/or their resolution

Political Developments

- Their political structure? How was it developed?
- What are the major parties? What are their differences?

Change

- How does change take place here?
- What things do not seem to change?

Religion, Religious Forms, Festivals, and Symbols

- Local religions of this area are: traditional, imported, or blended
- Level of Christian missionary activity
- How do the people worship and why?
- What are the major festivals?
- How is spirituality defined or understood?

What Is the History of Christianity in This Country?

- When was it introduced and by whom?

- How was it accepted? By whom? Why?
- If it has been commonly rejected, why?
- The most successful Christian churches or groups here, and why?
- Forms of indigenous Christianity and their history

The Adventist Church in This Country
- What is the history of the Adventist Church in this country?
- When was it introduced and by whom?
- Who has generally accepted or rejected it and why?
- Ways the church has been most successful?
- How does the local Adventist church relate to the world church? Why?

For information regarding SDA work in a specific country, see the *SDA Encyclopedia,* and do not forget to consult the valuable collections of the Adventist Heritage centers; for statistical information check the General Conference archives and statistics website (www.ast.gc.adventist.org).

Resources for Area Studies
The Internet has revolutionized how we locate information. The following sites can help you find materials for the area where you are going.

Internet Resources
www.lonelyplanet.com This site allows you to select a destination (country or city) and get very up-to-date information. Also, great facts-at-a glance feature.

www.embassy-finder.com Available in English, Spanish, French, German, and Chinese.

www.travel.state.gov The US State Department site is very informative on all countries of the world: for example, customs regulations, contacts and locations of embassies, safety/security, travel warnings, passport and visa information, and international adoption.

www.mislinks.org MisLinks has become the gateway for mission information of interest to missionaries, mission teachers, researchers, and leaders.

www.cia.gov/library/publications/resources/the-world-factbook/index.htm Information on geography, people, government, economy, communication, transportation, and military issues of any country can be found in *The World Factbook*.

www. adventistarchives.org Contains information of the General Conference Archives, the newest *SDA Yearbook*, and the World Church Statistics database originally developed by our office (Global Research Center) and now maintained by the GC.

www.cdc.gov This is the site of the Centers for Disease Control and Prevention. It provides a listing of disease and health topics for any destination country.

You will also want to check out your host country's website.

Conventional library resources are still a great way to find a lot of information on many countries. Here are a few types of resources you should consult if you are near a good university or college library.

Encyclopedias and Almanacs
- *Britannica*
- *Information Please*
- *World Almanac*

World Country Information
- *Cities of the World*
- *Maps on File*
- *Operation World (2010)*
- *Times Atlas of the World*
- *World Christian Encyclopedia*
- *World Factbook*

Popular Series Titles That Begin With

- *Area Handbook Series of ...*
- *Cultural Atlas of ...*
- *Peoples of the World ...*
- *People Profiles*
- *Survey of World Cultures*

Specific Country Studies

There are many works devoted to specific countries. Do a subject search: MISSIONS-(Name of the country).

Works Organized by Ethnic Groups (People Groups)

Various organizations have produced materials on the people groups of the world. The most complete series thus far is *People Profiles*, produced by Adopt-a-People Clearinghouse and other groups, such as Frontier Missions Centre of Australia.

Religions, Missions

Look for books on world faiths in the religion section of your library. The standard reference is the *World Christian Encyclopedia: A Comparative Study of Churches and Religions in the Modern World*, 2nd edition, (2001), edited by David Barrett.

Operation World (2010) is an 800-page Christian mission almanac in paperback—an inexpensive and rich resource.

Other works include

- *Eliade Guide to World Religions*
- *Encyclopedia of Modern Christian Missions*
- *Unreached Peoples Directory*
- *Atlas of Global Christianity*

Adventist Resources

For Seventh-day Adventist (SDA) reference materials you may want to consult the following items:

- *SDA Encyclopedia* (two vols.)
- *SDA Yearbook*
- *Statistical Report of the General Conference of SDAs*
- SDA journals published by different fields and institutions
- The Department of World Mission at Andrews University (269-471-6505)
- The Institute of World Mission (301-680-6711)

Your Turn

Going to the Local Market or Mall

To really connect with a community, go to the local market or mall for two to three hours. Spend the first hour observing, listening to conversations, and mapping the area. Attempt to blend in as much as possible and not stand out. Take brief notes unobtrusively and enlarge on them later. The second and third hour ask questions, continuing to listen and observe. Finally, record your reflections in your field journal.

The Physical Layout

- Where is the site located in relation to the neighborhood and other businesses? Is it easy to get to by car, or by public transportation?
- How much space is devoted to parking? Why?
- How are the stores arranged? Which stores are nearest to the entrances and the exits? What stores are missing? Why?
- What are the window displays like? What age, gender, and style

are most prominent in the displays? What sounds make up the atmosphere?

The Social Relationships

- What are the different social groupings? How do they interact? Do they mix?
- What kind of relationship can you observe? How is this different than where you have lived?

The Value System

- What values are reflected by the things you observe? What seems to have high or low value? How is this indicated? What social values are reflected in the relationships you see?
- List all the positive and negative aspects you observed.
- What implications could these observations have for your mission? For example, are there possibilities for ministry in this site? How might kingdom values interact with the observable local values?

Observe and Reflect

Use all your senses in your observation. Listen to the voices, noises, sounds, the music, and eavesdrop on conversations. Take in the smells. Taste the foods. Then ask yourself about the meaning of the things you see, hear, smell, and touch. What specific evidences do you see of God at work here? How can you become part of God's presence in this place?

For more information on doing an ethnographic study, check our website (www.instituteofworldmission.org).

Chapter 26

What to Do in Case of Emergency

Here you are—almost at the end of this book. Ready to go! But before you rush off, there's one more important thing we'd like to mention— your safety. No one wants to think about bad things that could happen, but the reality is that we live in an unsafe world. Hurricanes, earthquakes, typhoons, and other natural disasters happen everywhere. Illness or accidents are a part of life, and crime is a problem wherever there are people. Finally, in many places political unrest may lead to kidnapping, evacuation, and other difficulties.

Though few missionaries encounter serious problems of this nature, nevertheless, it is important that you think about them and know what you will do if anything like this occurs while you are serving. In fact, you want to do everything you can to live aware of your surroundings in order to prevent problems whenever possible (see How to Survive on the Streets on the next page).

The following guidelines have been prepared by the Mission and the General Conference of Seventh-day Adventists, and are the official guidelines for missionaries to follow in emergency situations. Please read them carefully.

Types of Emergencies

When we talk about emergencies, we mean the following types of events:

- Medical Emergencies: accidents
- Hospitalization: injury, illness
- Natural disasters: tsunamis, earthquakes, typhoons
- Political crises: war, coup d'état, terrorism
- Evacuation
- Death of a family member or co-worker

How to Survive on the Streets

If you are not accustomed to urban life, you may feel very uncomfortable in cities. Even cities in your own culture are likely very different from suburban and rural cultures. Here are some suggestions to help you survive in a city.

- Each city has its own "tempo" or "rhythm." It takes a few days to adjust to the new rhythm, so expect to feel "out of sync" for a time.
- Avoid carrying large purses or clutch purses. Purses should be hung over the body, not the shoulder.
- Separate your credit cards and driver license from your cash. If you are robbed, you only lose the cash.
- Look and act confident. Frightened people are a natural prey.
- Don't stare at people. In general, avoid eye contact on the streets.
- Avoid traveling alone, where possible.
- Avoid dark, empty streets.
- Avoid walking around the city at night.
- Women should never get into a taxi alone, especially at night.
- Generally, do not give money to beggars. (But always have a few coins for street musicians—they enhance life.)
- If you think you are being followed or feel uncomfortable, step into a store or shop and browse while you gather your bearings. If you feel seriously threatened, ask to use a phone to call the police.
- Subways are generally well lit and safe.
- Remember that most urban people are very normal, friendly, and willing to help you. Don't be afraid of everybody.

Things Everyone Must Do Before Anything Happens

- Register with your country's embassy or consulate, or register with the embassy that handles business for your country. Carry the contact number for that embassy. This is a must!

- Choose a person outside of your country (preferably a family member) who will be the contact person for you and your family. Be sure that your liaison persons at the GC, your home division, your host division, your union, and/or mission have the number of this person in case you can't get through to them in time of crisis.

- Know your line of communication within your country/mission/union in case of a serious crisis, and how to make an international phone call.

- If your institution includes several families, choose one person to be a crisis coordinator, who will make key decisions and contact the "outside world" in case of a serious crisis. That person should have the homeland contact numbers for all missionaries from your institution/compound so that they can with one phone call get the word out to one person who will then notify everyone of your status. (It would actually be good if your group chose one "person in the homeland" who has all the contact phone numbers for your entire group. This is a valuable precaution in the event that you can get only one short phone call out.)

- If possible, get to know people at your country's embassy or consulate and also one or more of the international news agencies. A few friends "in high places" can be very helpful in time of crisis.

- Keep all important documents (e.g., passports, ID cards, a few travelers' checks or a credit card, some hard currency, local government travel documents, visas, work permits, etc.) and important phone numbers (GC crisis hot line, one family contact person, local mission, union and/or division) together in a place that is easily accessible in case of a crisis. Remember: You may be looking for them in a state of panic and under very difficult circumstances.

- Keep ID emergency contact numbers and travel insurance info with you at all times.
- If you have short-term volunteers or independent missionaries working in your area even for only a few weeks, be sure the correct embassy, the local crisis coordinator, and the organization above you (mission, union, or division) know they are in the country.
- If you are in a sensitive area, it would be well to develop some discrete code language for use in a crisis.
- For each member of the family make a list of essential items to carry (no more than will fit in one small bag per person) in case you must pack in a hurry (e.g., prescription medications, glasses, contact lens solution, irreplaceable pictures, minimal clothing, baby formula, child's comfort blanket, etc.).

**Things You Should Do in Case of Serious Illness
or Accident Requiring Hospitalization**

- Notify and regularly update your liaison person at the GC and your host division so that they will know firsthand the extent of the problem. (This avoids rumors, speculation, and unnecessary worry.)
- If you are responsible for other missionaries (especially student missionaries or other volunteers), be sure to notify the organization that sent them and if appropriate, their parents.
- Keep a record of pertinent details in regard to the illness/accident, which you can share with family members so that they have a sense of involvement and an understanding of the situation. This is very reassuring to them when they are far away.

**Things to Do in the Event of a Crisis Requiring Evacuation
or Possible Evacuation**

- If communication with the "outside world" is still possible, get advice from the GC and/or the host division personnel assigned to advise you. Remember, they will be in contact with the US State Department (or its equivalent in the other divisions), the embassies of the countries involved, as well as international news agencies and will therefore usually have a reasonably good understanding of the overall seriousness of the situation. Listen to the advice they give! When they say "go," it is definitely time to go! Don't put the local or world church, or the local people or institutions, in jeopardy by insisting on staying when it is no longer safe–for you or for them.

- If communication with the "outside world" is cut off, try to get the most reliable advice available via shortwave broadcasts from out of the country, your country's embassy or consulate, international news persons, and church leaders at the host division and union levels.

- Try to work through your crisis coordinator to avoid confusion.

- During times of crisis keep your important documents with you at all times so that you can leave the country at any time and from any place, if it should become necessary.

- During times of crisis keep a small suitcase packed at all times containing absolute essentials so that you could leave at a moment's notice if necessary.

- If possible, have several people in your group keep a log of events leading up to, during, and after the crisis. This type of information may be very valuable at a later time as the event is evaluated locally as well as globally. The log should include phone calls, a chronology of events, times, places, dates, and possibly names.

However, due to the sensitive and sometimes dangerous nature of such issues, a person's name in a log kept by a foreigner could put them in serious jeopardy, so in most cases it would be better to refer to people in some kind of code which would not get them into trouble if it were to fall into the wrong hands.

- In your log, include the good things that happen as well as the bad so that when it is all over, those who were helpful can be properly recognized and thanked.

- Gather any information the local people may have of the event. Avoid any contact that may endanger them, however. Other missionaries and nationals may be able to get information through their normal contacts better than you can.

- If a witness can make a statement, take it. Get it in writing. If the person cannot sign it or needs to remain anonymous for safety, you write it, describing the informant as "a 50-year old farmer" (or use coded language). Then you sign it as receiving the testimony of this witness, date it, indicating your location.

- Keep in touch with the local (national) church authorities as well as other missions and churches in the area. Keep a record of their intervention.

- In the event of the disappearance of a missionary, keep a record of where the person lived and worked, the area where he or she was taken, the area where last seen, etc.

What to Do if You Are Abducted

- Remain calm and follow instructions. Do not give your abductors cause to hurt you. Appear cooperative and be polite. Do not argue with or provoke your captors. Listen carefully to their initial demands to make sure you understand what may be demanded of you. The first few moments of a hijacking and kidnapping are the most dangerous to the victim.

- Anticipate denial and disorientation, followed by depression during the early days of your captivity. You may suffer sleep loss and intestinal disorders as well. These symptoms of anxiety will recede if you are able to reduce stress and adapt to captivity.

- Adapt to dealing with your abductors in a respectful—but not subservient—manner. Attempt to establish some type of personal relationship with your captors. Win their respect and sympathy. It is not necessary to grovel and plead or demean yourself in any way. Do not lose faith in yourself. Remember, you did nothing wrong! They are at fault, not you. Tell them about your family. Show pictures, if possible.

- Avoid discussion of politics or religion, particularly politics. If your captors wish to talk about their cause, hear them out, but without indicating agreement or disagreement. If asked for an opinion, say that you are not knowledgeable enough to comment.

- Eat, rest, and exercise as much as possible. Keep your physical and emotional strength as high as possible. Try to avoid depression and always keep in mind that law enforcement officials are doing everything possible to end your ordeal. Exercise by stretching in place or by rolling your neck and limbs. Sleep and wash up when you can and eat and drink when you get the chance. Think thoughts of your family, pray, sing to yourself. Do not give up.

- Do not be disturbed by the Stockholm syndrome, that is, strong positive feelings toward your captors, if it occurs. It is common, normal, and may help improve chances for a healthy survival. This phenomenon is named for a bank hostage situation that took place in Sweden. During the course of the ordeal, the victim began to display strong positive feelings for the kidnapper. This is not a problem and, fortunately, not permanent. The malady is very common, particularly in long-term hostage situations. When it occurs, the captors usually take note of it, and experience shows that they are less likely to harm the victims.

- If you have a clear opportunity to escape, take it; but be mindful that your abductors may have laid a trap for you. Statistically, your best chances lie in a negotiated release. The FBI advises that escape should be a "last-resort" activity and is extremely dangerous.

- In the event of a rescue attempt, lie on the floor with your hands on your head, do not move, and shout your name. Expect to be treated roughly by your rescuers.

- Remember that everything possible is being done to secure your safe release. Keep a positive frame of mind.

- If your captivity is lengthy, it is imperative that you establish regular mental and physical exercise routines. If space is provided, walk daily and do in-place exercises. If you are confined in close quarters, do isometrics or in-place stretching exercises. Keep a mental calendar of what has happened to you. Do problem-solving. Make up a story or write a novel in your mind about your experience. Even daydream!

Dealing With Terrorism

Terrorism around the world is on the increase, and since terrorism cannot always be avoided, we need to know what to do if and when it occurs.
- Maintain a low profile. Do not flaunt your nationality.
- Dress conservatively, seek to blend in locally.
- Always be polite, but not servile.
- Be alert for unusual activity in airports or other public places.
- Don't seek danger.
- In case of violence, keep close to the floor.
- Avoid congested areas that might be targets.
- Be sure someone knows where you are and knows your schedule.
- Do not put others in jeopardy by disregarding evacuation orders.
- Do not talk politics or religion with strangers.
- Commit your life to Jesus and rest in His hands at all times.

Things to Do in the Event of the Death of a Missionary

When there is death by non-violent causes (no "foul play" involved)

- Get an autopsy, if it is deemed appropriate.
- Notify the embassy/consulate of the person's home country.
- Notify the GC and the family contact person(s).
- Follow the recommended procedures in organizational policy.
- Get the necessary permission to either bury in the local country or send the body back to the home country, depending on the family's wishes.

When there is death by violent causes

- Get an autopsy, if possible, with a complete report on cause of death, the type of wounds, injuries, etc.
- If an autopsy is not possible, get one or two doctors to examine the body. If they are afraid to be named, have institutional leaders or another expatriate (preferably one with a medical background) witness the examination, sign, date, and note the place.
- Document, as far as possible, the actual events leading up to the death.
- Follow the same procedures as in a non-violent death (see above).
- Submit a report of the case as you know it that includes
  - Specific cause of death (bullet wounds, stabbing, strangulation, massive beating around head or vital organs, etc.).
  - Specify the nature of the wounds, (e.g., where the bullet or bullets entered the body, where they left the body, caliber of bullets).
  - Specify how many wounds.
  - Take pictures or draw diagrams to help clarify the nature of the wounds.
- Look for additional evidence at the scene (bullet casings, etc.).
- Ask press representatives who are there to send pictures to division and/or GC officials as deemed appropriate.

- Have a mission representative (expatriate) hand-carry a preliminary medical exam or autopsy out of the country with the photos to the division or General Conference.
- Anything that would be needed as forensic evidence (e.g., clothing, etc.) should be hand-carried in a plastic bag out of the country to wherever it will be analyzed.
- If possible, notify the international press so that they can tell the story to the world accurately.
- Send a copy of the autopsy report, documents, and photos to the appropriate embassy in the country of death.

If necessary, enlist the help of embassy officials and/or the government of the deceased's home country (including legislative bodies) to help see that justice is carried out. The denominational administration should send copies of the autopsy/medical report, duplicates of the photos and the denomination's "official version" of what happened to the appropriate government officials, asking for a full report, if deemed necessary and helpful.

Special Roles at the Time of the Crisis

The role of institutional leadership:
- Notify your embassy
- Notify next highest institutional level or General Conference office
- Notify family (unless done by next highest level)
- Notify local (national) church authorities
- Notify local civic authority (police, etc.)

The role of the crisis communicator:
- Notify contact for international network
- Notify international press representative

The role of General Conference or appropriate division office:

- Notify families
- Notify the appropriate denominational channels

Contact your State Department or Foreign Affairs Office

- If an investigation is needed, you may need to contact the appropriate office in your State Department or Foreign Affairs Office responsible for your area of service.

Some of this material was adapted from materials by Sean M. McWeeney of Corporate Risk International, and from "Managing Terrorism Risks" by the Ackerman Group.

An excellent resource on safety issues is C. Rogers, & B. Sytsma. 1999. *World Vision Security Manual: Safety Awareness for Aid Workers.* Geneva, Switzerland: World Vision.

Chapter 27

Tips for Travel

In this book we have tried to prepare you for your mission adventure. If you have come this far, you are probably seriously considering an assignment somewhere. You have done your area studies and know what climate to expect when you arrive and have found other helpful tips from travelers that have been there before you. So now it is time to think about your own traveling and packing. To help you, we have put together a few tips to consider as you prepare for your trip.

General Packing Suggestions

Almost everybody over packs, but then, what is a luxury to one is a necessity to another. The list below is not prescriptive but descriptive. Your list will differ from that of others, as it reflects your personality and needs. Before packing, be sure to check current government security regulations and your airline's luggage policies.

- Wear a hidden pouch instead of a purse or backpack to safeguard your money, credit cards, passport, etc. Wear it in front, not in back.

- In case your checked luggage gets delayed, always take a carry-on bag (small backpack, day pack, or small roller bag) packed with necessary medicine, toiletries (in sizes allowed), something to sleep in, and a change of clothing and underwear.
- Keep camera equipment, computers, and other valuables in your carry-on luggage.
- Packing folded clothes in large plastic self-sealing bags keeps them clean, dry, and organized. Take an extra plastic bag to hold dirty items while you are traveling.
- Put luggage tags both on the outside and the inside of your suitcase.

Traveling by Air

Most of you will be traveling to your mission assignment by air. Air carriers differ in luggage allowances, check-in policies, and other details. Check with your travel agent or the airlines directly for the current rules and regulations for all the different airlines you will be using. You will probably also want to review the historical and cultural information you have collected on your country of destination.

- Make sure you have your passport and health certificates in a handy place, as well as the necessary visas.
- Make copies of (a) your plane ticket or e-ticket receipt, (b) at least the first two pages of your passport, and (c) the international phone number of your credit-card company. Keep a copy in a separate place in your luggage and leave one copy with someone at home. This will make replacement much easier should it become necessary.
- Make sure the proper people know your itinerary: parents, spouse, children, supervisor, destination hosts, etc.

Sample Packing List

- ✔ Toilet gear
- ✔ Small scissors and/or nail clippers (not for carry-on bag)
- ✔ Prescription medicine
- ✔ Small sewing kit (pick one up at your next hotel)
- ✔ Collection of safety pins
- ✔ Medical kit, including clean syringe and needles
- ✔ Alarm clock
- ✔ Minimum sets of underwear, socks, and other necessary clothing
- ✔ Extra pair of shoes
- ✔ Swiss Army knife (not for carry-on bag)
- ✔ Shortwave radio
- ✔ Small flashlight
- ✔ Nylon cord for clothes line or tying boxes, etc.
- ✔ Self-closing plastic bags, different sizes
- ✔ Inflatable pillow and eye mask for sleeping on planes
- ✔ Set of electrical adaptors and small transformer
- ✔ Dual-voltage appliances as needed
  (e.g., hair dryer, travel iron)
- ✔ Extra batteries for radio, clock, flashlight

- Prearrange for desirable seats. People who do not do this often sit in the middle seat, between very large neighbors, fighting for a spot for their elbows to rest. Also, prearrange for vegetarian or other special meals.
- When staying over en route, verify your next flight as soon as you arrive.
- Plan to check-in at least two hours before domestic flights and two three or more before international flights. Ask someone knowledgeable about the local airport for the best time to check-in at that airport. Also factor in traffic congestion when planning traveling time to the airport.

Suitcases

- Check with your airline for what you are allowed to check in and carry on. Security regulations around the world are variable and often stringent. In some places your carry-on luggage may be weighed.
- Don't put pocket knives or other sharp objects into your carry-ons.
- Avoid expensive, designer luggage and fancy name-tags. Attaching an inexpensive color band helps you to easily identify your luggage.
- Hard-sides may be slightly more difficult to break into. Soft-sides will stretch for add-ins.
- Most airlines allow one carry-on bag and a personal item, such as a purse or computer case.

Dressing for Travel

- Dress comfortably in loose clothing with a jacket or sweater in case the plane becomes cold.

- Taking your shoes off in the plane may make you more comfortable. Make sure to stay well hydrated and take frequent walks to help keep your feet from swelling. For long-distance travel, wear compression socks.
- Consider your destination when you dress for travel, particularly when you cross the equator.
- If you're buying new clothes, buy wrinkle-free or crinkled fabrics.
- Take things that can be worn at least two or three different ways.

Other Considerations

Money and Valuables

- Take a limited amount of hard currency (e.g., €100) in small notes.
- Use credit cards with appropriate caution. ATMs generally offer the best rates and lowest charges for cash.
- Avoid sidewalk money-changers. Even local people are sometimes cheated out of hundreds of dollars and not know it until much too late.
- Be careful not to flaunt cash, expensive watches, cameras, or other valuables in public. Pickpockets abound!

Safety Factors

- Be cautious about opening your hotel door to strangers or hotel employees you have not requested for service.
- Avoid walking alone in dark cities.
- Avoid driving after sundown.
- Be thankful for airport security people. Don't complain and never joke or argue with security personnel.
- Avoid getting into a taxi alone at night.
- Females should avoid traveling alone if possible.

Computers

- Be alert for computer thieves, especially at security check points.

- Keep your batteries charged on your electronic devices so you can turn them on if requested at the security check.

- If you have to check your carry-on at the gate be sure to take out your computer and keep it with you.

International Calling Cards and E-mail

International telecommunications change quickly, so do some research before you go.

- Generally international calling cards are far less expensive than regular phone services.

- If you want to use your e-mail abroad through your internet service provider, make sure you check out your options before you leave. The local Seventh-day Adventist leaders may also be able to assist you in many places, since many use e-mail to communicate internationally.

Chapter 28

Coming
Home

I remember coming home from my first mission trip. What a life-changing experience it had been! I had been in an unbelievable country: beautiful, poor, and confused. I was confused too. I had strange stories to tell. I had met amazing people and immense needs. I had gained new perspectives. There, one dollar could pay for one month's rent. Ten dollars could pay an engineer's monthly wages. Now I felt guilty indulging in an ice-cream cone for a dollar. As I observed the seemingly careless way in which we spend our money at home, I also felt angry.

This experience is common for those who return from mission service. The longer you lived abroad and the better you adjusted to your host culture the more acute you may feel the symptoms of reverse culture shock when you return home. Once home, you will have opportunities to share your unique story. How to do that well is one of the topics in this section. In this chapter we help you think about life after your term of service.

 **Think About It**

- Have you thought about what will happen when you return home from your mission assignment?
- Have you heard other missionaries talk about their experience of coming home?
- What are some of the things you remember?

Re-entry

So you are on your way home. Soon you will see your loved ones and your friends. There are so many experiences to share with them. You are also looking forward to going out to your favorite restaurant. Just thinking about being home soon fills you with excitement.

Then you are home. Everybody is there to admire you and to listen to your amazing stories—at first. But soon the excitement is over. People are busy going about their lives. And home is not quite what it was when you left. Life has gone on while you were away, and now it is your turn to fit in again. You discover something you did not expect. Something else has changed. It is you!

Reverse Culture Shock

Now that you have experienced a different way of life you suddenly see the contrast with the way of life in the homeland: the endless rush, the schedules, the materialism, the superficiality, and many other things. Things you had taken for granted, now seem wrong. What do you do? We all experience a range of emotions during the period of readjustment. What is crucial is not to get stuck in the negative ways of reverse culture shock.

Turtle—A common response is to get frustrated and critical of people who don't seem to care about the world out there or care about mission. Their "stupid" questions ("Do people in ... really use no toilet paper?") may irritate you. So you may be tempted to just withdraw into your protective shell.

What to do—Remember there is no way they can possibly share your level of intensity of feeling and commitment. You now have an "active understanding" of another way of life that can't be accessed without the experience of actually living in another culture.

Crusader—You may try to force your experience on people and to convert them to your viewpoint. You become a crusader for change in your home, your church, your community, your country, or your culture.

What to do—Remember that just as you are entitled to live your life the way you choose, you must allow other people to make their own choices. You may go through both "stages." Eventually you will adjust.

Adjusting to Being Home

One thing that helps with adjustment is to view your home culture as another "foreign community" that you must approach as you approached your host culture. Your mission experience has pushed the boundaries of your awareness and given you perspectives that you can't get through books or talking to international students at home. To reap the benefits from your mission experience you can do several things.

- *Evaluate your experience*. It is important that you take time to reflect on your experience. What did you learn? How have you changed? What will you do now?

- *Share your story*. One of the greatest benefits of a mission experience is how you can influence your friends and family with a new commitment to missions. Mission multiplies as those who went out tell their stories to those at home. What is important is to tell it well.

- *Stay involved in mission.* Your mission experience may only be a first step for God to reveal to you what He has planned in your life. Be attentive to his leading.

For many missionaries the cultural adjustment pains in reentry are as unsettling as the culture shock first experienced when going out. So don't despair. A good resource for dealing with reentry issues is Storti, C. (2001). *The Art of Coming Home.* Yarmouth, ME: Intercultural Press.

Tips to Improve Your Story

Record stories—Keep a journal to help you remember concrete details. The sounds, smells, sights, and conversations will quickly be forgotten without it.

Be ready—People who remember that you went "somewhere" will politely ask, "How was your trip?" Use the occasion to share a one-minute summary of your experience. Use a short story.

Take initiative—Arrange for settings where you can share your experience. Sabbath school, youth meetings, and prayer meetings are good settings to focus on the mission situation you have known.

Speak up—A story told well in a clearly audible voice will be appreciated. Practice diction. Speak as clearly as possible. Don't be guilty of not communicating your excitement just because your voice could not be heard.

Start strong—In your opening, aim at arousing faith with curiosity. Never start with an apology. Try to create anticipation.

Paint verbal pictures—From your opening statement move into the story with vivid details so your audience can visualize the scene (the squeaky chair, the smell of incense, children splashing in a puddle, your own feelings at the time). Select important things. Answer the basic five questions: who, what, where, when, and why. But don't overdo it. Be careful with jargon you picked up while on your trip that your listeners are not familiar with.

Illustrate your story—Dramatize. Act out a conversation. Include facial expressions and verbal inflections. Use your pictures to illustrate. But be sure to select only quality pictures and to keep them moving fairly quickly and in the sequence of your story. Don't just flash pictures on the screen with a running commentary. Using an object may be appropriate when making a point.

Focus on people—Mission is people sending people to reach people. Stories that touch the hearts of listeners are stories of people. Programs, plans, and policies are important, but they are here to serve people. In your stories and pictures, focus on people, their faces, thoughts, and emotions.

Convey important lessons—Stories can hold the attention of an audience. But remember you are not there to merely entertain. Every experience of life can serve to illustrate some biblical principle. A brief statement ("You can't outgive God!") or a quotation from Scripture ("And the greatest of these is love!") is helpful. But don't belabor the point.

Accentuate the positive—It is important to relate the challenges you have faced in a hopeful spirit. Rather than condemning people for their materialism, challenge them to see the tremendous opportunities to invest in the Lord's work around the world. Don't bemoan your trials. A little humor can help, for example, "my isolated conditions were not the end of the world but I could see it from there."

Encourage interaction—Give opportunity for questions. Good communication is a two-way street. Listen to the questions. Answer specifically. Don't feel threatened. You have an answer for every question. It may be, "I don't know." Supportive comments, such as "That's a good question," or "Did you catch the significance of Jack's comment?" set a good tone.

Stop on time—Remember that if you are back in a culture where time is of supreme importance, you may often be asked to give a "short report."

Don't despair. Just give a *Reader's Digest* condensed version of your story. Be careful not to go beyond the time limit, and you may be asked again!

To sum it all up: Don't miss the opportunity to tell your story. God used people with a story like Hudson Taylor or the Adventist pioneer missionary John N. Andrews to spark modern missionary movements.

Based on Blue, R. and Gibson, T. (Eds.). (1992). "Tell the Story: How to Communicate with Others When You Return." In *Stepping Out: A Guide to Short Term Missions* (pp. 180-182). Seattle, WA: YWAM.

Now What!?

Here are a few ways to keep your missionary experience alive:

Share your mission experience with others. Don't try to give everybody who asks you about your mission experience a long detailed report. But be prepared to go beyond the stereotype "I had a great time!" and try to share some brief, concrete, personal stories that illustrate what you learned.

Ask your pastor for time to briefly share your experience with your church. Sabbath School is an ideal time to share some of your pictures, videos, and stories with your church. If you have taken time to think through your mission experience, you will be able to select those aspects that help your fellow church members understand why mission is still important and how everyone can get involved.

Contribute to the world mission report in your church. Even the weekly mission report can become a way to stay involved. A mission story related by someone who had a firsthand taste can be an effective contribution to keep mission alive on the local church level.

Support others preparing to go on a mission assignment. Your experience can be a valuable resource to other missionaries.

Increase your mission offering. This is a tangible way you can support the mission of the Adventist Church. Remember that the general mission offering often provides the funds to keep those projects running that got started by special one-time offerings.

Learn foreign languages. One short-termer returned from Russia and decided to learn the language in order to communicate more effectively the next time he went to Russia.

Continue to study the people and culture of your host country or other culture that you might serve in the future. Many universities provide studies in international issues. Cross-cultural experience enables you to study more empathetically and respond to important issues more appropriately.

Get involved in local community ministries. Our eyes are often more open to mercy ministries when we have lived in poor areas of the world. Christ's mission included the healing of the whole person. Most communities, especially in urban areas, provide many opportunities for Christian social service.

Consider getting involved in short-term or long-term missionary service. Many long-term missionaries started their mission career as a short-term volunteer. Some mission agencies such as ADRA consider short-term experience the doorway to more extensive mission involvement. And, many permanently returned career missionaries enjoy staying involved in mission through short-term mission trips.

Adapted from Eaton, C., & Hurst, K. (1991). *Vacation with a Purpose.* Colorado Springs, CO: Navpress.

Your Turn

1. The following seven questions can assist you in evaluating your experience when you have returned from your mission service. You

may want to do this with a friend who has shared your experience or by yourself.

- What did you like best about your mission experience?
- What was the worst thing that happened to you?
- What is the most significant lesson God taught you during your mission service?
- In which area of your life did you see the greatest changes?
- What one experience sums up what God did through you?
- What is the biggest challenge you face in returning home?
- What things are you most thankful to God for?

2. As you think about sharing your story, review the tips for better communication in this chapter. Outline a short report you could give, keeping in mind the principles you learned in this chapter.

3. As you think about the future, what are some of the things you plan to do to stay in touch with your experience and continue your involvement in mission?

Part 6 Resources for Further Study

Chaplin, M. (2015). *Returning Well: Your Guide to Thriving Back Home After Serving Cross-Cultural.* Newton, MA: Newton.

Jordan, P. (1992). *Re-entry: Making the Transition From Missions to Life at Home.* Seattle, WA: YWAM Publishing.

Knell, M. (2007). *Burn Up or Splash Down: Surviving the Cultural Shock of Re-entry.* Downers Grove, IL: InterVarsity.

Pascoe, R. (2000). *Homeward Bound: A Spouse's Guide to Repatriation.* Vancouver, BC, Canada: Expatriate Press.

Storti, C. (2001). *The Art of Coming Home.* Yarmouth, ME: Intercultural Press.

Promises for Missionaries

Exodus 4:12 "Now go: I will help you speak and will teach you what to say."

Deuteronomy 31:8 "The Lord himself goes before you and will be with you; he will never leave you nor forsake you. Do not be afraid; do not be discouraged."

Deuteronomy 33:25 ". . . And your strength will equal your day."

Psalm 27:1 "The Lord is my light and my salvation—whom shall I fear? The Lord is the stronghold of my life—of whom shall I be afraid?"

Psalm 46:10 "Be still, and know that I am God; I will be exalted among the nations, I will be exalted in the earth."

Psalm 56:4 "In God, whose word I praise, in God I will trust; I will not be afraid. What can mortal man do to me?"

Psalm 118:6 "The Lord is with me; I will not be afraid. What can man do to me?"

Proverbs 3:23, 24 "Then you will go on your way in safety, and your foot will not stumble; when you lie down, you will not be afraid; when you lie down, your sleep will be sweet."

Isaiah 12:2 "Surely God is my salvation; I will trust and not be afraid. The Lord, the Lord, is my strength and my song; he has become my salvation."

Isaiah 40:31 "But those who hope in the Lord will renew their strength. They will soar on wings like eagles; they will run and not grow weary, they will walk and not be faint."

Isaiah 51:5 "The islands will look to me and wait in hope for my arm."

Isaiah 55:4-13 "See, I have made him a witness to the peoples, a leader and commander of the peoples. Surely you will summon nations you know not, and nations that do not know you will hasten to you, because of the Lord your God, the Holy One of Israel, for he has endowed you with splendor.

Seek the Lord while he may be found: call on him while he is near. Let the wicked forsake his way and the evil man his thoughts. Let him turn to the Lord, and he will have mercy on him and to our God, for he will freely pardon. 'For my thoughts are not your thoughts, neither are your ways my ways,' declares the Lord. As the heavens are higher than the earth, so are my ways higher than your ways and my thoughts than your thoughts.

As the rain and the snow come down from heaven, and do not return to it, without watering the earth and making it bud and flourish, so that it yields seed for the sower and bread for the eater, so is my word that goes out from my mouth: It will not return to me empty, but will accomplish what I desire and achieve the purpose for which I sent it.

You will go out in joy and be led forth in peace; the mountains and hills will burst into song before you, and all the trees of the field will clap their hands. Instead of the thornbush will grow the pine tree, and instead of briers the myrtle will grow."

Jeremiah 1:7, 8 "Do not say, 'I am only a child.' You must go to everyone I send you to and say whatever I command you. Do not be afraid of them. For I am with you and will rescue you."

Matthew 6:33, 34 "But seek first his kingdom and his righteousness, and all these things will be given to you as well. Therefore, do not worry about tomorrow, for tomorrow will worry about itself."

Matthew 24:14 "And this gospel of the kingdom will be preached in the whole world as a testimony to all nations, and then the end will come."

Matthew 28:20 "I am with you always—even to the ends of the earth."

Mark 9:23 "Everything is possible for him who believes."

Mark 16:17, 18 "And these signs will accompany those who believe: In my name they will drive out demons; they will speak in new tongues; they will pick up snakes with their hands; and when they drink deadly poison, it will not hurt them at all; they will place their hands on sick people, and they will get well."

Luke 11:9-10 "So I say to you: Ask and it will be given to you; seek and you will find; knock and the door will be opened to you. For everyone who asks receives; he who seeks finds; and to him who knocks, the door will be opened."

Luke 11:13 "If you then, though you are evil, know how to give good gifts to your children, how much more will your Father in heaven give the Holy Spirit to those who ask him."

Luke 18:27 "What is impossible with men is possible with God."

John 14:12 "I tell you the truth, anyone who has faith in me will do what I have been doing. He will do even greater things than these, because I am going to the Father."

Acts 1:8 "But you will receive power when the Holy Spirit comes on you; and you will be my witnesses in Jerusalem, and in all Judea and Samaria, and to the ends of the earth."

Romans 8:28 "And we know that in all things God works for the good of those who love him."

Romans 8:35-39 "Who shall separate us from he love of Christ? Shall trouble or hardship or persecution or famine or nakedness or danger or sword?.... No, in all these things we are more than conquerors through him who loved us. For I am convinced that neither death nor life, neither angels nor demons, neither the present nor the future, nor any powers, neither height nor depth, nor anything else in all creation, will be able to separate us from the love of God that is in Christ Jesus our Lord."

1 Corinthians 15:58 "Therefore, my dear brothers, stand firm. Let nothing move you. Always give yourselves fully to the work of the Lord, because you know that your labor in the Lord is not in vain."

2 Corinthians 4:8, 9 "We are hard pressed on every side, but not crushed; perplexed, but not in despair; persecuted, but not abandoned; struck down, but not destroyed."

Philippians 4:13 "I can do everything through him who gives me strength."

Philippians 4:19 "And my God will meet all your needs according to his glorious riches in Christ Jesus."

Hebrews 13:6 "The Lord is my helper; I will not be afraid. What can man do to me?"

Promise Psalms

Psalm 23 "The Lord is my shepherd, I shall not be in want."

Psalm 46 "God is our refuge and strength."

Psalm 91 "He who dwells in the shelter of the Most High will rest in the shadow of the Almighty."

Special Promises for Dealing With
Giant Obstacles and Challenging Circumstances

Exodus 23:27–33 "I will send ... ahead of you and ... make your enemies turn their backs and run. I will send the hornets ahead of you to drive (them) out of your way ... until you ... take possession of the land."

Deuteronomy 1:29 "Do not be terrified; do not be afraid. . . .The Lord you God, who is going before you, will fight for you... "

Deuteronomy 3:22 "Do not be afraid . . . the Lord your God himself will fight for you."

Joshua 23:5 "The Lord your God himself will drive them out of you way. He will push them out before you, and you will take possession of their land, as the Lord your God promised you."

Joshua 13:6 "I myself will drive them out."

Joshua 17:18 "Though [they] have iron chariots and though they are strong, you can drive them out."

Isaiah 45:2 "I will go before you and will level the mountains; I will break down gates of bronze and cut through bars of iron."

Miscellaneous Mission Thoughts

"We are asked to do an impossible task, but we work with Him who can do the impossible."

    J. Hudson Taylor

"How often do we attempt to work for God to the limit of our incompetency rather than to the limit of God's omnipotency."

    J. Hudson Taylor

"All God's giants have been weak men [and women] who did great things for God because they reckoned on God being with them."

    J. Hudson Taylor

"God's best gifts are not in things but in opportunities."

    Unknown

"We have all eternity to tell of victories won for Christ, but we have only a few hours before sunset to win them."

    Jonathon Goforth

"All that He takes, I will give.
All that He gives, I will take."

    Mabel Williamson